BBC Books, an imprint of Ebury Publishing
One Embassy Gardens, 8 Viaduct Gardens, London, SW11 7BW
BBC Books is part of the Penguin Random House group of companies whose addresses
can be found at global.penguinrandomhouse.com

This book is published to accompany the television series *Strictly Come Dancing*,
first broadcast on BBC One in 2004. This series (Series 22) first broadcast 2024.

Executive Producer: Sarah James
Series Director: Nikki Parsons
Series Producer: Jack Gledhill

With thanks to: Victoria Dalton, Jasmine Fox, Harriet Frost, Jack Gledhill, Kate Lawson,
Rose Sammut, Nora Ryan, Kate Wilkinson, and Eve Winstanley.

First published by BBC Books in 2024

www.penguin.co.uk

A CIP catalogue record for this book is available from the British Library

ISBN 9781785949388

Project Editor: Céline Nyssens

Printed and bound in Italy by Elcograf S.P.A

The authorised representative in the EEA is Penguin Random House Ireland,
Morrison Chambers, 32 Nassau Street, Dublin D02 YH68.

Pictures © BBC Photo Archive

2025 Annual

BOOKS

Contents

Soap Star to *Strictly* Champ

Ellie LEACH

Her bubbly nature and gleeful grin won the hearts of the nation as she danced her way to the *Strictly Come Dancing* Final and lifted the Glitterball trophy. But it was no act for former *Coronation Street* star Ellie Leach – she was having the time of her life.

'*Strictly* put a smile on my face, one hundred per cent,' she says. 'I loved being at *Coronation Street* and, being me, I smiled a lot offscreen, but my character, Faye Windass, had a hard life, so viewers rarely saw me happy. *Strictly* was a once-in-a-lifetime opportunity and it was great to show my fun side. It's been the best experience.'

Although she triumphed in the Grand Final, Ellie's mind was not on the prize when she entered the competition, but rather on learning Latin and ballroom.

'*Strictly* is a show I love watching and always wanted to be a part of, so I was just grateful to be in it. I never even thought about winning. I just wanted to learn a new skill and enjoy myself each week, however long I was there. The fact that it lasted right up until the end, and we actually won, was surreal and something I never imagined.'

Paired with Vito Coppola at the launch show, Ellie was thrilled – but no one was happier than her mum! 'When I first met Vito, before we knew who we were partnering, we immediately got on,' she says. 'Everyone was lovely, welcoming and kind, but I instantly gelled with Vito and we buzzed off each other. Also, my mum loved him and kept saying, "I hope you're dancing with Vito." I knew I'd be happy, regardless, but Vito immediately made me feel comfortable. He's like a puppy, always excited, but with him I feel calm.'

While the Manchester-born actor is naturally 'shy' when she first meets someone, she soon came out of her shell, and Vito helped her confidence grow on the dance floor as well.

'Vito is a big personality, but when I warm up to people I also have a big personality, and we brought out the best in each other. I think we worked so well as a team because he understood me.

'Over the course of the series, I grew so much in confidence. I was nervous for the first live show, but I was happy with how our week-one Quickstep went, and even though I'd only known Vito for two weeks, I already knew I could rely on him and he would always be there for me. He was so supportive.'

Ellie worked hard to learn the routines and believes the turning point came in week five, with a

dramatic Paso Doble to 'Insomnia' by Faithless. The routine earned the couple their first 10 and a huge score of 37 from the judges, with Motsi calling it a dance on 'a whole different level'.

'Vito says he saw a switch in me in our Paso Doble,' says Ellie. 'We'd done a Jive, Foxtrot, Viennese Waltz and Samba, but the Paso is completely different, and Vito told me, "I need to see your serious, fiery side." I wasn't sure I could bring that side of me out, but it was a turning point because I threw myself into something different and really enjoyed it. It became one of my favourite dances.

'As a couple, our favourite was the American Smooth, which we danced again in the Final. I absolutely love the glitz and glamour of it. It's very Hollywood and very *Strictly*.

'I also loved Blackpool, when we danced the Charleston. The rehearsal week was amazing. We had so much fun and laughed all day, and the dance really showed our personalities when Vito and I are

together. We are silly. We turn into mischievous kids when we're around each other and that's what the Charleston was.

'What's wonderful about doing different styles and a different dance each week is that every dance has distinct memories. When I hear a song I've danced to, I go over the steps and remember what an amazing time I had during the rehearsals and performing it live on Saturday.

'Both the American Smooth and the Charleston saw the couple top the leaderboard with a near-perfect score of 39, with Craig praising Ellie for the 'best cross-swivel ever' in the Blackpool routine. They paved the way for the spectacularly close Grand Final, where the couple beat Bobby Brazier and Dianne Buswell and Layton Williams and Nikita Kuzmin to the crown.

'Winning the Final was a blur,' she says. 'The whole night was an emotional whirlwind because we had a little hiccup with the showdance and then danced our American Smooth, knowing it was our last dance, but I was really proud of everything I'd done. I felt so lucky to have gone through the competition and reached the Final, so to lift the Glitterball was completely unexpected. I was shocked.' Ellie's friends and family, especially *Strictly*-superfan mum Karen, always believed Ellie could do it; she says they had 'more faith in me than I have in myself'.

'In everything I do, not just *Strictly*, I want to make my family and my friends proud, and as long as I do that, I've achieved what I want to achieve,' she says. 'My parents, sister and best friend were in the audience that night and were over the moon when we won. The rest of my family were watching in the local pub and were screaming and crying. They videoed their reaction so I could watch it and I felt like I was there with them, which was amazing.'

After their series triumph, Ellie and Vito joined the *Strictly Come Dancing* Live Tour, further bonding with their co-stars on the road. 'It was a completely different experience to the TV show and I loved it,' she says. 'In our industry, you might cross paths, but on *Strictly* you are sharing the experience with a news presenter, a tennis player or an Olympian. Where else could I say I danced on the same floor as Angela Rippon?! It's amazing.

'My bond with Vito is one of the biggest things I'll take from *Strictly*. He was the best friend throughout and still is. He will always be in my life and I feel like I won just having him as a partner, teacher and teammate.'

As *Strictly* champion, Ellie has truly found her feet and hopes to keep dancing in the future.

'Dancing is something that brings joy into people's lives, and it has brought so much joy into mine. It changed my life, which sounds dramatic, but it genuinely did. I'm so grateful to have been a part of *Strictly Come Dancing*. It's been a whirlwind, the most perfect experience, and dancing has made me so happy.'

Sarah HADLAND

Comedy star Sarah is fulfilling a life goal by signing up for *Strictly Come Dancing*, having been an avid viewer for 20 years, and she is raring to get on that dance floor.

'I'm so excited,' she says. 'I've been a massive fan from the get-go, and I've been asked to do it before but it hadn't felt like the right time because of other work. But I think there's a moment when everything aligns and you just have to say, yes, this is my year to do it.'

The actor and comedian is best known for her role as Stevie in the BAFTA-nominated sitcom *Miranda* and as one of the original cast of *Horrible Histories*. She was nominated for an RTS Award for Best Comedy Performance for her leading role in *The Job Lot*, which ran from 2013 to 2015, and also appeared in the 2008 Bond movie *Quantum of Solace*.

As she slips on her dancing shoes, Sarah will be cheered on by a group of celebrity superfans who have been egging her on to take the *Strictly* challenge, including comedy co-star Miranda Hart. And she admits she had to employ her impressive acting skills to keep the secret after agreeing to take part.

'We have a big WhatsApp group, which includes Patricia Hodge, Clare Balding, Emma Freud and Sue Perkins, and we all watch the Final at Miranda's house every year,' she reveals. 'You're not allowed to talk during the dances and it's very serious. I knew it had been mooted that I would be taking part as far back as last Christmas, and there have been other get-togethers with Miranda and everybody else saying, "Sarah should do it. Why isn't Hadders doing it?" But I already knew I *was* doing *Strictly*, so I was quite pleased with myself because I completely game-faced it, saying, "You always say that. Not this year." When it broke, they were all saying, "How could you?" But they're really thrilled and excited for me.'

With her mum and her best friend already bagging tickets for the first show, Sarah says her friends and family are all desperate to see her on the dance floor.

'The minute people found out I was doing it, they went bananas,' she laughs. 'Everybody I know has messaged to say they want to come. I'm going to have to have a ballot between my friends and family. I don't know how I can get them all in. My mum is super-excited. I'm scared what my mum might do on the night – she might end up on the dance floor.'

Dancing with reigning champion Vito Coppola, Sarah has found getting the posture right in the early days of training harder than she thought.

'When I watch at home, I look at the TV, saying, "Get your elbow down. Why is your finger up?" When you come to do it yourself you suddenly realise how tricky it actually is. They put your hand in one place, then the shoulder has to be in a certain position, the head has to go back and you're trying to remember to smile. All that's fine as long as you don't expect me to dance as well!'

One of the things she is most looking forward to is being *Strictly*-fied. 'I'm up for everything,' she says. 'The dresses, the tan, the glitter, the nails, the hair, the lashes – I want it all! Everything is really thrilling, full of pinch-me moments, like the first time I stood at the top of the staircase. When you've been a fan of the show that's so exciting. I'm going to enjoy every minute, because to be part of a show that people love so much, and which makes people so happy, is a real privilege.'

Reigning champion Vito Coppola is bursting with energy as he approaches his third series on the show – but he's met his match in dance partner Sarah Hadland.

'Sarah is so happy and has such a high level of energy,' he says. 'Usually I'm like the puppy bouncing around the room, but this is the first time I have been paired with someone who is more active than me. I'm having to slow her down on the steps because she's too quick for a Quickstep! It's amazing because she's so full of joy and so energetic.

'Sarah is so funny. She makes me laugh all the time and she is so excited. Every morning we both arrive at rehearsals with a big smile, and at the end of the day we leave each other happy because it has been a productive day. We're having a good time.'

The *Miranda* star has appeared in musicals in London's West End, but Vito says the ballroom and Latin discipline requires different skills, and his new pupil is eager to learn.

'Sarah is well coordinated, but she had never done any ballroom or Latin, so we have to start from the beginning,' he says. 'The stamina you need for dancing is completely different from any other activity. To dance properly needs strength, effort and commitment, and getting the technique and detail right is difficult. It's not easy, but we are on point and it's going really well.'

Born in Salerno, Italy, Vito comes from a dancing family, with a gymnast mum and a dad who ran a dance school. He was Italian champion at nine and is a three-time World Championship finalist and European Cup Winner. In 2021, he won Italy's *Ballando con le Stelle* (*Dancing with the Stars*), and a year later he made the Grand Final of *Strictly Come Dancing* with Fleur East. Last year he lifted the Glitterball trophy with actor Ellie Leach.

'Sometimes I can't believe it actually happened,' he says. 'I was very happy, and if I watch the video, I still get emotional. But for me, it's all about the journey. I told Ellie, "You were my winner since day one, whatever happened." So we were very happy and excited to win, but it was just the cherry on the cake.'

As Vito dances his way into the new series, he insists the win hasn't changed his approach.

'I like to take every new journey from a blank page, so I'm not approaching this series differently. I'm super excited, happy and grateful about the past two beautiful years with both Fleur and Ellie, but this new series is a blank page because it's another partnership, another series. I just want to make sure Sarah has the best time, because *Strictly* is a once-in-a-lifetime experience and you need to live it to the full.'

Vito COPPOLA

Two
DECADES
of DANCE

Tess Daly and
Bruce Forsyth, 2004

Natasha Kaplinsky and Brendan Cole,
the first winners of *Strictly Come
Dancing*

With a splash of glitter and the now-familiar fanfare of the theme tune, *Strictly Come Dancing* burst onto our screens on 15 May 2004. Presented by Tess Daly and the late, great Sir Bruce Forsyth, the new weekend entertainment show drew from the long-running ballroom series *Come Dancing* and added celebrities into the mix, with eight competing in the first run and newsreader Natasha Kaplinsky bagging the first ever Glitterball trophy.

Over the next two decades *Strictly Come Dancing* became an international phenomenon, often under the name *Dancing with the Stars*. Since those first steps on the dance floor, the show has evolved and grown, with each year bringing bigger, better dances and fabulous new pairings. But Anton Du Beke – one of four original cast members along with Craig Revel Horwood, Tess Daly and singer

Tommy Blaize – believes the heart of the show remains the same.

'I watched the first show again recently and it's extraordinary,' says Anton. 'It has remained true to itself with the dancing and the couples, but it's incredible how it's changed. When they announced us, in series one, I came down one staircase and my partner came down the other, then we joined at the bottom. There were only eight of us. The dancing has evolved – we have lifts and other moves we never had in those early days, and extra dances like the American Smooth, Charleston and Salsa, where you can showcase incredible choreography – but the heart of it remains the same, which is very important. It is still the most wonderful thing. It still fills me with huge amounts of joy and excitement.'

Anton du Beke and partner Lesley Garrett, photographed for the first ever series of *Strictly Come Dancing*

West End director and choreographer Craig joined the judging panel, alongside Len Goodman, Arlene Phillips and Bruno Tonioli, and remembers the screen test that landed him the job. 'I watched a monitor of couples doing ballroom and Latin dances and then had to critique them. Initially, they said my answers were a bit long and asked me to shorten them. Then they asked me to sum up one dance in three words and I said, "Dull, dull, dull." Those were the first three words out of my mouth on the show.'

Anton remembers being consumed with excitement ahead of the first show, and never more so than when he met his great hero, Sir Bruce

Forsyth. 'I met Brucie for the first time at the press launch and I was speechless,' he says. 'For anybody who has known me for the last 20 years, that's quite a state for me. I never find myself speechless!'

With two series in the first year, in the spring and autumn, the show captured the heart of the nation, with the first Grand Final pulling in an audience of almost 10 million.

The full cast of series one

'Len and I always said that we gave it three weeks,' laughs Craig. 'Of course, we were wrong and it worked brilliantly. Suddenly it just took off and our viewing figures were going up and up. I think the nation fell in love with it.'

For the judges and dancers, being centre stage on a weekend television favourite was an instant game-changer. 'I never thought about the consequences of viewers watching it and that suddenly people would know my name,' says Craig. 'One moment I was nobody and then overnight, when I was

The original *Strictly Come Dancing* judges, photographed in 2004

walking in London, truck drivers were tooting their horns, shouting out what I'd said, and people were stopping me in the street. Over the 20 years my own catchphrases – like "Fab-u-lous", "A-maz-ing" and "Dance Disaster" – have even been turned into ringtones.'

Anton adds: 'We dancers were all very excited on the first show, but TV wasn't our business, so we thought we'd do this for a few weeks, then carry on with our normal lives. Little did we know that it would change our lives forever. You could even argue that I met my wife through *Strictly* because I was invited to a celebrity do and she was there as a guest. Everything about my life changed. It has been the most incredible thing to have happened to all of us involved in the show, for which I'm forever grateful.'

Originally broadcast from the BBC Television Centre in West London, *Strictly* moved to its current home at Elstree Studios in 2013. Technological advances have also seen the routines enhanced with LED lighting, projections that set the scene for each dance, and even augmented reality, which has had comedian Bill Bailey dancing with an elephant and pop singer HRVY trapped in a snow globe.

Craig says. 'It's certainly grown in style and glamour. The introduction of the new dances, as well as bringing in Street and Contemporary through the Couple's Choice, has meant a wider variety of styles. The production values are amazing, with incredible lighting and wonderful projections, so it's gone from strength to strength.'

The show's success has also inspired the nation to dance. Craig says, '*Strictly* shows that dancing is for everybody and everyone can do it.'

With an audience that spans all generations and sees friends and families gathering together on weekend evenings, *Strictly* has built up its own army of superfans. '*Strictly* fans are special people and their devotion and dedication to the show is fantastic,' says Craig. '*Strictly* is proper family entertainment and brings people together from all different walks of life, and that's what is so amazing. It is a show that a three-year-old can watch with their 93-year-old great-grandmother. It brings the community together and makes dance accessible to everybody. There's no other show that does that.'

Anton agrees that the fans of the show are 'the most important people. They are why we do it and they're the ones who really own the show. I always maintain the BBC make the show, but it really belongs to the public. We want them to be involved and invested and we want them to vote, so we're making it for them. *Strictly* is joyous and there are so many layers to it, from the frocks, the dances, the live music and the singers to the journeys of the celebrities. You feel like everything's okay in the world when *Strictly* is on.'

Craig's most iconic moments

Jill Halfpenny's series-two Jive
'That was the first time I'd ever got the 10 paddle out. There were no 10s in series one and I didn't give any 10s until the Final of series two, but that dance set the bar high and it was amazing.'

Ed Balls's Salsa
'Ed Balls doing his "Gangnam Style" Salsa with Katya Jones was brilliant. It truly showed off his personality and it was so entertaining.'

Rose Ayling-Ellis's Couple's Choice

'Rose's routine to Clean Bandit's "Symphony", where the music fell silent and she carried on dancing, was absolutely fantastic. It was a huge moment, incredibly moving, and won the BAFTA for the Must-See Moment of the Year, which was well deserved.'

Ann Widdecombe's Samba

'The Samba with Anton in the yellow dress was hilarious. I can still look at that and laugh, and she took on the show with great humour.'

Angela Rippon's leg extension

'When Angela Rippon did that incredible leg lift, it was a real "wow" moment. At 79, she was just incredible.'

The Mark Ramprakash moment

'When Karen Hardy and Mark Ramprakash's microphones got tangled in series four, Brucie really came into his own. He was fabulous. He was dancing with the sound engineer, doing all sorts of things to distract the audience. It was hilarious but also showed what a pro he was.'

Bill Bailey's series-18 Couple's Choice

'Bill was brilliant to watch but his street dance, to "Rapper's Delight" by the Sugarhill Gang, is one that definitely sticks in the mind. I thought that was fantastic.'

John Sergeant's series-six Paso Doble

'The sight of John Sergeant dragging Kristina Rihanoff in the Paso Doble is one I'll never forget. It's gone down in the annals of *Strictly* history.'

My *Hello, Dolly!* moment

'In 2019, we did a Musicals Week routine that ended with me playing Dolly Levi, from *Hello, Dolly!* I climbed up on top of the cake and sang the final two lines. I love that!'

Bruno's fall

'Bruno falling off the chair after telling Lisa Riley, "I love the comedy ending," is a classic moment. I did an impression of him falling off it when he was away one week as well.'

Teethgate

'After Anton's Austin Powers routine with Emma Barton, in series 17, I mentioned his "fake teeth" — only to be told they were his own. It was a cringeworthy moment but also hilarious. Luckily, Anton saw the funny side!'

Anton's most iconic moments

Sir Bruce Forsyth routine

'The number-one memory for me is doing "Me and My Shadow" with Brucie, my great hero. Performing alongside him was a great honour. That's always been my most treasured moment.'

First ever dance

'The Brucie moment is closely followed by the first dance I danced with Lesley Garrett, in series one. I rewatched it recently and it brought back lovely memories. Coming out and doing the very first show was a very exciting moment for me.'

Series-13 Final

'My most memorable moments are usually the ones with me in them! Making it to the Final with Katie Derham was great. It was the first time I'd been in a Final and it was wonderful.'

10s with Emma Barton

'Getting 10s with Emma Barton was fabulous. We got two 10s for our American Smooth in Blackpool and went on to get more for our Charleston before going into the Grand Final, which was great.'

Falling for Ruth

'One of the funniest memories for me was falling over with Ruth Langsford during our series-15 Paso Doble. I fell on my back and Ruth rolled on top of me, which was a brilliant moment.'

Rose's silent dance

'The most iconic moment on *Strictly* for me is the incredibly moving Couple's Choice from Rose Ayling-Ellis, with the silent segment. It really made me emotional and, as I said at the time, it was the greatest thing I've ever seen on the show.'

Dancing Partners

'There were many memorable dances with Ann Widdecombe and I loved every one. I have loved dancing with all my partners. Judy Murray was brilliant and Nancy Dell'Olio was incredible.'

Head Judge Shirley is like a 'cat on a hot tin roof' in anticipation of the new series and says she can't wait to bring some Saturday-night glitz into the nation's living rooms.

'I'm looking forward to a little bit of sparkle on those dark winter nights,' she says. 'And of course we're celebrating the show's twentieth anniversary, which is wonderful, and the executives have worked very hard to bring us yet another incredible series of *Strictly Come Dancing*.'

After a long break without seeing her fellow judges, Shirley is looking forward to the reunion. 'I've missed them terribly. As soon as we are together, the four of us will catch up. There will be lots of cuddles with Craig and Motsi and plenty of mischief from Anton. It will be fabulous.'

Always the epitome of glamour, the former Latin champion is planning to revamp the wardrobe this year – thanks to a stylish *Strictly* colleague.

'Motsi and I have already been chatting about our wardrobe, and this year, we'll be wearing lots of power suits,' she says. 'My son Mark adores Claudia Winkleman, and he thinks she's got the best dress sense he's seen for years so I should take a leaf out of her book!'

With over four decades of dance experience, competing, teaching and judging, Shirley has a keen eye for a potential finalist, but she's not picking anyone out too soon.

'There are a lot of movers and shakers this year and I wouldn't like to pick a winner early because they're all fabulous.

'I'm hoping they all have an amazing work ethic and I know all of them will win the hearts of the public, but the competition always throws up the unexpected so you can never predict a winner. I've got my eye on everybody!'

Through her own career in the dance business, Shirley has made lifelong friends and has watched many of the professional dancers grow up – so she is delighted to see two of them returning to the *Strictly* floor this year.

'Seeing Amy Dowden back on the floor will be wonderful,' she says. 'I'm going to need a box of tissues because I know this is a huge milestone for her, and one she's been fighting for.

'I've followed Aljaž Škorjanec's career from when he was a juvenile under-12 competitor. He brings great energy and great work. It's going to be absolutely fabulous to have both him and Amy back.'

Picking her favourite moments from the last series is difficult, Shirley says, because there were 'so many great numbers'.

'I'll never forget seeing Ellie and Vito fregolina and farol in the Paso Doble – that's an extremely difficult and technical step and it was wonderful to see them pull it off. Krishnan and Lauren's "Boom Shack-A-Lak" Cha-cha-cha will be forever engraved in my mind, too!'

Shirley is now hoping the class of 2024 can reach the dizzy heights of last year's Final.

'The Grand Final was absolutely spectacular,' she says. 'Our champion, Ellie, was a very deserving winner. You know why? Because the public picked her – and I never argue with the British public!'

Shirley BALLAS

Shayne WARD

He's been a chart-topping singer, an actor and soap star, now the multi-talented Shayne Ward is hoping to add dancer to his list of achievements – and he's taking inspiration from a few screen legends.

'I love the idea of dancing, and dancing has always been part of the family,' he says. 'I'm dancing all the time with my little girl and my son, but whether it's good or not is another question. I've always had this belief that I am John Travolta or Patrick Swayze when the jukebox is on, so that's what I'm channelling.

'I really want to do the dramatic dances, like an Argentine Tango, because the vision I've got in my head is Antonio Banderas dancing with Catherine Zeta-Jones in *The Mask of Zorro*. I'd love to do something with such intense passion.'

After winning the second series of *The X Factor* in 2005, Shayne scored a Christmas number one with the single 'That's My Goal', as well as topping the UK charts with his self-titled debut album. In 2015, he joined ITV's *Coronation Street* as Aidan Connor, a role that earned him Best Newcomer at the National Television Awards and Best Storyline at the Soap Awards, among others. On stage, Shayne starred in *Rock of Ages* in London's West End, and most recently he has played former police detective Jack Grayling in the crime series *The Good Ship Murder*.

The Manchester-born actor, who is paired with Nancy Xu, follows in the footsteps of many former *Corrie* co-stars, including Kym Marsh, Catherine Tyldesley and current champion Ellie Leach.

'Ellie was fantastic, and hopefully I will get to keep that Glitterball trophy up North,' he says.

Coming up to the first live show, Shayne admits to a few nerves, but he sees that as a positive. 'You're going to feel nerves, but that's natural and it's great to have them. You should get nervous because this is out of your comfort zone, but you want to do well, you want to make your mum who's watching at home proud. I'm more excited at the moment.'

One of the highlights so far has been trying on the outfits for the show, and Shayne, dad to Willow, seven, and two-year-old Reign, is not the only one of the family keeping a close eye on the costumes and taking tips from Designer Vicky Gill.

'Everything looks amazing, and when you step into the costume you instantly feel like you're halfway there,' he says. 'Now I just have to get one foot in front of the other!

'The kids are super excited. My little girl's eight in December and wants to be a dress designer. I think she's more excited about the dresses than me dancing, but if she's happy, Daddy's happy.'

Although no stranger to live TV, Shayne says he's been surprised by the public support he has got, even before he has taken his first step. 'You don't realise how big the show is until you're actually in it,' he says. 'After the cast announcements, we were being patted on the back like we've done the most incredible thing just to be in it. I knew it was loved, but just how much it is loved has completely blown my mind.'

Nancy Xu is partnering actor and singer Shayne Ward and says she is still 'buzzing' with excitement over the pairing.

'I genuinely feel grateful to have a dance partner for another year and to be able to dance on *Strictly Come Dancing*,' she says. 'And I can't tell you how pleased I am to have Shayne as my partner. It's early days and we need to get to know each other better, but I think we have a good natural connection, which is a gift. He wants to give it everything and do the best he can. I feel blessed.'

Coming from a musical background, the past *X Factor* winner is likely to have rhythm and understand tempo – qualities Nancy believes could work to his advantage.

'When you're teaching, you often have to help people with counting the bars, but Shayne knows music, he loves music, and he can understand what I'm talking about when I say I want him to feel the rhythm. I don't need to explain. In fact, he might teach me more about music, too.'

Nancy began dancing at eight in her native Huaihua, China, and has travelled the world competing. She was runner-up at the 2013 International Singapore Championships, third place in the 2010–2012 CBDF National Amateur Latin Championships and a finalist in the U21 World Championships in 2010. On her twenty-eighth birthday, in July 2019, it was announced she was joining *Strictly*. She has since reached the semi-final with both Rhys Stephenson and Will Mellor, and last year partnered comedian Les Dennis.

'Les is lovely,' she says. 'He very much threw himself into the game and he was very entertaining. But in rehearsal, he was really focused and very serious. He said to me, "I will try my best, try to entertain and give as much as I can."'

Hoping to make the Final this year, Nancy says she can see Shayne going all the way, but she is not counting her chickens.

'We will take it step by step,' she says. 'After all, there are still four months to go!'

Looking forward to taking part in the twentieth-birthday celebrations, Nancy believes this year has added magic for several reasons – not least the return of fellow professionals Amy Dowden and Aljaž Škorjanec.

'This year was already special before we even knew the celebrity line-up, because we have Amy and Aljaž back in the family,' she says. 'So for our audience, there's already something to look forward to, as well as the twentieth-anniversary celebrations.

'Since the first day I joined, I have seen the whole show develop in terms of the different types of performances. Every year, there's something viewers can expect to see and look forward to. The incredible team who work on the show try to find new ways to make the show even better and wow the audience, so fans can always count on *Strictly Come Dancing* being fabulous.

'I genuinely think this year the whole cast is amazing. At the launch show we could see that. *Strictly Come Dancing*'s twentieth-anniversary year is going to be incredible.'

Nancy Xu

Nancy Xu 25

Wynne EVANS

As an opera star, Wynne Evans has an ear for music and has starred in many stage shows and now he can't wait to learn some moves.

'Strictly is the best show ever and I've been watching it for years,' he says. 'Also, I've been on a bit of a weight-loss journey and I thought learning to dance would be a good way of continuing that and trying to get super-fit, so I'm looking forward to doing more training. I'm looking forward to the costumes. I'm also really looking forward to the musical arrangements, because I think Dave Arch and his team are amazing. I'm looking forward to pretty much everything.'

Wynne became a household name after starring as Gio Compario and later himself in the catchy Go Compare adverts. Born in Carmarthen, Wales, Wynne trained at the Guildhall School of Music & Drama and the National Opera Studio, and has enjoyed a distinguished 25-year career, which includes two number-one classical music albums as well as being principal player at major opera houses around the world. He has also performed over 200 times at the Royal Albert Hall in London. Wynne currently has a daily radio show on BBC Radio Wales and has previously had shows on BBC Radio 3 and Classic FM.

Having performed live all over the world, Wynne is hoping his stage background will help him combat the nerves.

'I'm used to the live element, but I'm well trained at opera singing so I can keep my composure,' he says. 'I think that composure goes out the window when you're doing something that you're not trained to do. I've always found the middle of a stage – no matter how many people are watching – to be quite a calming place, because I know what I'm doing, but I think that could change. But I'm definitely going to try and combine my love of opera into one of my routines.'

As a ballroom and Latin novice, Wynne is keen to try all the dances but he is especially enthusiastic about one Austrian classic.

'I've sung in a lot of Viennese concerts, especially the famous New Year's Day ones, so I'm looking forward to the Viennese Waltz,' he says. 'Although the more I see of it, the more difficult it looks.'

Throwing himself into the training, Wynne says his recent fitness regime is helping with the stamina.

'The training is full-on but it's great. I run every day anyway, so I'm really enjoying it, I've got to say.'

Looking fabulous also means the famous makeover, but Wynne says the classic ballroom style is de rigueur for an opera star. 'I've worn tails pretty much all my career, so I'm used to wearing those,' he explains. 'The glitter? Maybe not so much! But I'm enjoying it, I'm going with it. Everything they ask me to wear, I'm up for it.'

As a proud Welshman, Wynne is kicking off his Strictly journey with a Samba to a Tom Jones track, and he can't wait to show partner Katya Jones the sights of his homeland.

'I'm determined to give this my all and I aim to make Wales proud,' he says. 'And I want to show Katya a bit of Wales and give her the full Welsh experience.'

Asked about his signature move, Wynne reveals the one 'dance' he tends to do at parties – although it's unlikely to make it onto the Strictly dance floor. 'It's called the Slug,' he laughs. 'It's like the Worm but less energetic. In fact, it's practically static!'

Former *Strictly Come Dancing* champ Katya Jones is entering her ninth year on *Strictly* and is hoping her partnership with opera singer and radio presenter Wynne Evans will be beyond 'compare'.

'I was so surprised when I was paired with Wynne, but we got on like a house on fire instantly,' she says. 'He's really joyous, with lots of laughter, and I think he's got some moves. He messaged me after we met saying how glad he was to be dancing with me because he had watched me with Ed Balls and Tony Adams and told me, "If you can make them dance, I really hope you can make me dance, too!"'

Katya believes that as a celebrated singer and stage performer Wynne will have some useful skills to bring to the dance floor.

'He is used to playing characters and translating emotions to the audience, whether it's happy, sad, crying or laughter, because as an opera singer you're an actor as well,' she says. 'He's got so much charisma. He wants to entertain people and he's got all the ingredients for that, but he genuinely wants to learn to dance. Even when we were having photos taken, he made sure his foot was pointed. He wants to absorb as much information as possible while entertaining the audience. I'm impressed with his attitude so far.'

A proud Welshman, Wynne was over the moon to be told their first dance would be to the Tom Jones song 'Help Yourself', says Katya.

'I revealed to him on the launch show that we were doing the Samba, but at that stage they don't really know what that means,' she says. 'But when I said we would be dancing his first dance to another Welsh legend, Tom Jones, that made his *Strictly* experience already. Being a Welshman, that means a lot to him.'

Katya is three-time World Amateur Latin Champion and four-time undefeated British National Professional Champion. She joined the show in 2016, making an unforgettable debut with Ed Balls, and won the Grand Final with Joe McFadden a year later. Other partners have included boxer Nicola Adams and swimmer Adam Peaty, and last year she reached the quarter-finals with Nigel Harman before he was forced to withdraw because of injury.

'Nigel was so talented and I loved dancing with him,' she says. 'We were able to be so creative together. Each dance was really like storytelling. I'm very proud of each one of our dances.'

Looking forward to the next series, Katya is thrilled to welcome back fellow professionals Aljaž Škorjanec and Amy Dowden, and says the launch show was an emotional reunion. 'We did a special group dance for Amy and she was dancing with Aljaž,' she says. 'The whole room was filled with emotion. It was such a special moment.'

As a professional on the show for almost half of its 20-year run, Katya is delighted to be part of the birthday celebrations.

'I watched the first episode recently and nobody could have predicted that it would be so popular, so to be part of it 20 years later is very special,' she says. 'People still love it and the moment they hear that theme tune their faces light up with joy and happiness. I told Wynne, it's important to remember that on Saturday night, as soon as the *Strictly* theme tune plays, families are gathering around the TV to watch and enjoy the show. It makes so many people happy. I think it being its twentieth year is testament to that.'

Katya JONES

Strictly on SOCIAL

Advancing technology means it's not only on TV screens that fans can keep up with the world of *Strictly Come Dancing*. Social media gives viewers access to clips, updates and tons of *Strictly* fun wherever they are. Throughout the series, exclusive content is found across TikTok, Facebook, Instagram and YouTube, as well as on the *Strictly* website, with blooper reels, behind-the-scenes footage and dancers, celebs and judges getting up to some very jolly japes.

Digital Executive Producer Nora Ryan begins gearing up for the series in mid-July and is a crucial part of the unveiling of the new contestants in August, releasing the names onto social media platforms to coincide with the announcements in the mainstream media. 'There's a lot of audience expectation around the celebrity reveals,' she says. 'We're always looking at fun new ways to reveal our celebrities. For instance, this year we announced Gladiator Montell Douglas on the gaming platform Roblox, where she has her own in-game character, so that was really exciting.'

Once the celebrities are announced and raring to go, Nora and her team of four work tirelessly to make sure there's plenty to interest *Strictly* fans, starting with filming some early moves.

'When we film the title sequences with each couple, I go along, put them in front of a big green screen and direct them to do as much of each dance style as they can,' she says. 'At that point, they don't know any dancing, so the professional talks them through a couple of steps of a Tango or a Charleston and so on. Then, over the next 13 weeks, when the songs and the routines for the following week are revealed, we can put out footage of the couples giving a taste of their next dance.'

Once the series starts, content is released seven days a week. With currently 1.1 million followers on Instagram, 500,000 on TikTok and 1.3 million on Facebook, it's the biggest social campaign across the BBC, excluding sport, and last year *Strictly* videos were viewed an amazing 600 million times.

'We're embedded into the production, and we've got our own room in Elstree where we make content every Friday. We get 25 minutes to half an hour with each couple, so we might film one big video with a game or quiz, and smaller TikToks as well. The couples really enjoy it because it's a bit different and light-hearted fun.'

On Saturday, the team watch the dress run so they can begin to prep for the live show and write scripts for their clips. 'The one thing you never know, though, is what the judges are going to say or the scores they'll award, so we have to be reactive during the live show, but the dress run helps give us a guideline of what to look out for.

'During the show, we publish the clips from the routine on every platform, and then we add in the "door burst", which is where the couples come bursting through the glitter doors after their routines. The couples do a piece to camera for us, and it's great to get that immediate and direct backstage reaction. We then put the routine and reaction together and subtitle the social media clip, because accessibility for all our audience is really important.

'We not only share it on *Strictly* socials, we share it on BBC iPlayer and BBC social media accounts as well. We also collaborate with the celebrities and the professionals, so they can put any clips they want to use on their personal social media channels too.

'For the results show we put out clips of the opening professional dance and the guest music act, and, of course, the leaving moment for the eliminated couple, which is all-important for the audience. A few years ago we would have kept that back because people may not have wanted to know, but social media has changed so much that viewers want to know the result, so we put it out as soon as it happens.'

The stream of content continues throughout the week, with snippets from *It Takes Two* as well as exclusive features and fan favourites.

On Monday, for example, we have a video series on our social media channels called *Listening In* which has proved very popular with fans.

'The couples are wearing mics throughout the show, and while they are dancing we can hear the professionals giving their partner encouragement,' says Nora. 'They'll be saying, "You can do it," or counting the steps, and we take that audio and run it over the footage so you can hear what they were saying. There are some funny moments – Neil had a dance move called "granny's knickers", which we found out when we listened back to the mics. One I remember was Nikita offering Tilly Ramsay imaginary cucumber sandwiches as they walked onto the dancer floor in character at the start of one of their routines!"

'We're always jumping on other shoots that the main production are doing so that we can be as efficient as possible,' Nora says. 'Getting the early footage is a way of making the song-and-dance reveals sing, and the fans love them. They're really excited to see what dance the couples are doing, and if it's a really popular song they're dancing to, the social post gets even more clicks.'

On Wednesday and Thursday, the team put out footage from the training rooms. 'As we get closer to the end of the run, we also put blooper reels together,' says Nora. 'People really love the bloopers.'

Although the real work starts when the series begins, Nora spends weeks before that coming up with fresh ideas for content to work on through the series.

'I have the big ideas plotted through, but I also like to keep it reactive, so if something is trending, we can jump on that quickly,' she says. 'Also, themes come from the couples themselves, because we don't know what's going to come up when we start filming with them, so I don't like to plan everything too tightly. On social, it's easy to see what is doing well, what the audience is enjoying, so we can switch and do more of it.'

Nora's favourite shows are the themed weeks. 'I love Movie Week because everyone gets to be even more creative,' she says. 'The Barbie-inspired routine last year was amazing – the attention to detail was second to none. Before the routine was aired, we put out a backstage social post with Gorka and the rest of the male professionals, dressed as Kens, walking down the corridor, and he was miming to "I'm Just Ken", which wasn't in the dance. It was a great exclusive because the hair and make-up and costumes were so good that Gorka looked like Ryan Gosling.'

While Nora's team work hard all week, there's plenty of fun along the way.

'My favourite part of the job is coming up with a new idea and then seeing it all coming together and everybody enjoying it,' she says. 'I usually direct because I like to be hands-on and I love working with the talent. We are like a family, but everybody mucks in and everybody is up for doing whatever we ask. It's fun and they enjoy it as well. There's always a lot of laughter in our room.'

Tasha GHOURI

TV trailblazer Tasha Ghouri sprang to fame as *Love Island*'s first ever deaf contestant, but being asked to star in *Strictly Come Dancing* is her 'dream come true'.

'I'm so excited. I can't believe it's actually happening,' she says. 'There's no feeling to describe it. I've been watching the show since I was little and it's a firm Ghouri family favourite, so I know it's going to be an unforgettable experience. I just hope I can represent and make everyone proud out on that dance floor.'

Born in Thirsk, Yorkshire, Tasha has been a passionate advocate for the hearing impaired all her life. She started her career as a model and first came to attention when she was featured in an earring campaign, which showed her cochlear implant. In 2022, she appeared on *Love Island* and made the final. Using her platform to promote the learning of sign language, she amassed a following of over 2.2 million on social media. Tasha has since worked with the Government's Department of Education to champion issues pertaining to the deaf community. She has written a novel, *Hits Different*, and has her own podcast, *Superpowers with Tasha*.

Now she feels inspired in her *Strictly* journey by series-19 winner Rose Ayling-Ellis, the show's first deaf contestant.

'When I look at *Strictly*, it means representation. Rose was on there and she was absolutely incredible,' she says. 'To follow in Rose's footsteps means a lot to me. I'm doing this for myself and the deaf community, and for people who struggle with their confidence. I'm here to help them find self-love and confidence. To me, this is really about raising awareness and doing something for myself, because it's something I've always wanted to do.'

Although Tasha has worked as a dancer in the past, she's starting from scratch with ballroom and Latin. But she's keen to learn all she can from partner Aljaž Škorjanec.

'I'm trained in commercial dance, so knowing the music and having rhythm might help me,' she says. 'But in terms of ballroom-dancing styles, I've never done any of those before. I've never danced with a partner before so I'm having to restart and reset. In the first rehearsals there were moments it felt so odd, being in frame. It's a whole different ball game, and that's what I'm here for – to learn.'

As a keen viewer of the show, Tasha says her favourite routine of the past was Hamza Yassin's Salsa, which she describes as 'incredible' because it 'looked so joyous', but the dance she has set her heart on is the Tango.

'The Tango looks so passionate and so strong,' she says. 'You have to be very in the zone together, so I feel like that would be a really cool one to learn. But I think dancing on the ballroom floor, whatever the dance, is the most exciting part for me. Getting out there with my professional partner and dancing in the moment together will be such a buzz.'

Such is Tasha's joy at being in the show, she's even 'excited' to face the judges after completing her routines.

'I'll just take on the feedback – that's how you'll improve. I'm excited to meet them.'

As a former model, as well as a brand ambassador for numerous fashion names, Tasha is used to glamming up, but that hasn't dimmed her enthusiasm for *Strictly* sparkles.

'Being *Strictly*-fied is literally the bit I cannot wait for. We've already had some dresses made, and as soon as you put them on you just transition into someone else. You become a different personality, like your alter-ego. I love it!'

Returning to the *Strictly Come Dancing* dance floor after a two-year break, Aljaž Škorjanec could not be happier to be back.

'It feels great, and the launch show was amazing,' he says. 'The most emotional thing was that first time on the floor, dancing the group numbers with my fellow professionals. It was really great to be back in the room with so many people that I have done the show with for so long.'

Paired with Tasha Ghouri for the new series, Aljaž is also delighted to be back in the training room with a celebrity partner.

'I missed teaching my dance partners, making sure that they're comfortable and confident, and then seeing them excel on the *Strictly* dance floor.'

Aljaž was born in the small town of Ptuj in Slovenia and took up dancing at five. He is a 19-time Slovenian champion in Ballroom, Latin and Ten Dance. He joined *Strictly* in 2013, sweeping to victory with model and TV presenter Abbey Clancy in his first year. His previous partners have included Alison Hammond, Helen George and Daisy Lowe, and, in 2017, he made the Final again with actress Gemma Atkinson. He's hoping to add another Glitterball trophy to his cabinet in his returning year.

'Being paired with Tasha, I feel like I have won a lottery,' he says. 'She's really eager to learn and has a lot of respect for the craft.'

The reality TV star made a good first impression during early rehearsals, and her potential has Aljaž dreaming of some spectacular routines.

'With Tasha we'll be able to do some incredible choreography and storytelling. I'm really excited for the series. I can't wait to get back on the dance floor.

'I think Tasha's strengths will lie in trusting herself and trusting her own ability and using the confidence that I think she already has. *Strictly* brings out the best in you when you start performing on that dance floor, so I'm really excited for her to do that.'

As well as his own emotional return to the show, Aljaž was partnered with Amy Dowden for the group dance, welcoming her back after a year away through serious illness.

'Amy's an incredible, inspirational woman and I take my hat off to her and anyone ever going through what she's been through. I feel privileged to dance on the same floor. It's really special to have her back, and the dance was an amazing homage to her.'

Having taken a break to concentrate on being a dad, the seasoned professional is bursting to get back in the saddle. 'I'm looking forward just to being back on the *Strictly* dance floor and in the rehearsal room with Tasha.

'I think the first live show will be a full-circle moment. After stepping away for two years and coming back, I appreciate it and respect and cherish the opportunity to do this show in a completely new way, and I'm humbled by it all. I can't wait.'

Frocks
—AND—
FRILLS

Head of Wardrobe Vicky Gill and her team have created thousands of stunning costumes and, while styles and designs change over the years, some things remain constant.

'When we meet our cast members we're looking at them, their personalities, how they move. The building block for us is born from our cast members. It's a process, because as they grow on the show, their personalities grow, or maybe they're shy and we design around that. It's a movable feast.

'Today, the garments are a little less like traditional competitive ballroom dancing costumes, but there's definitely room for some of that tradition within the series. The volume we need for certain movements and looks to suit different dance styles – those core elements are still very much present, but we operate in slightly different ways depending on how the creative team want to move and shake with it.'

For Vicky, each dress or ballroom suit comes with the memory of a moment. 'Some might be slightly nervous moments and others are really quite emotional. I'm someone who stands in the back, enjoying the moment, watching everybody have fun. I love the show and it brings so much joy. It's great family entertainment, so it's great to be a part of it.'

Here, Vicky shares her thoughts on 20 of the most iconic outfits from the past 20 years.

1. Erin Boag's American Smooth with Colin Jackson

'This is one of the first dresses I designed for *Strictly* after I started working with original designer Su Judd, when I was working for a dancewear company. This dress is special in that respect. It was 2005, but I think it stands the test of time.'

2. Abbey Clancy's Cha-cha-cha

'Abbey Clancy always looks incredible, but I love the fun of this outfit. It was a very easy dress to design and she makes it look so amazing.'

3. Denise van Outen's Jive / Quickstep

'They did a week when the couples fused two dances, so the length of the skirt and the volume had to have that Fifties' vibe but also cross over and function between a Jive and Quickstep. I love the top fabric on this and the combination of the burgundy and the raspberry underskirt, the colour and shape of the dress.'

4. Bill Bailey's Couple's Choice

'I love this outfit because it demonstrates how, if tailoring is cut for dance, it assists the movement. In a regular high-street suit, the shoulders would be up around your ears. Bill was fantastic but also looked sleek from beginning to end, and that's down to the wardrobe team. We're using tricks like shirts attached to pants, braces or a figure-of-eight elastic in the jacket to make sure the shoulders stay down. There are lots of things happening inside to create a clean performance, so the garment doesn't become a distraction.'

5. Annabel Croft's Final American Smooth

'I loved creating this dress for Annabel. While silk is a delicate fabric not usually recommended for performance garments, it made the dress move so beautifully across the ballroom. We used honey, peach and sunrise crystals to give light and shade on the flesh-coloured section, sitting alongside crystals in mixed sizes for the strings around the neck and back of the garment.'

6. Kimberley Walsh's American Smooth

'I love the simplicity of the dress. Girls Aloud were celebrating their tenth anniversary and I think this number allowed her to feel like she was firmly a member of Girls Aloud but embracing the *Strictly Come Dancing* ballroom.'

7. Oti Mabuse's Samba with Danny Mac

'Some of my choices are based around moments in time. I love the detail on this dress. We created a skin-colour mesh base, and the crystals on this dress are a flat colour, so they are not giving reflection, just lines and a little bit of shine with the aqua, orange and cream definition on top. The dress, the performance and everything – this was just one of those moments when the stars aligned.'

8. Maisie Smith's Quickstep

'Maisie was such a little firecracker all series. What I like about this dress is the fabric, which we bought in. It's vertical strips of fabric with a slight flare in them, so it's like a waterfall, which runs down the dress and then combines with godets and a feather hem, giving a lovely texture. Maisie made the dress move and dance.'

9. Helen George's Halloween Samba

'Helen had lots of lovely looks across the series. Sometimes you get into the groove with what works with people's silhouette, shapes, personality and choreography. Samba is not an easy dance and to be doing it as a mummy made it fun. We all did our bit there to make sure that the entertainment value was 100 per cent bang on.'

10. Angela Rippon's Cha-cha-cha

'This was the first costume we created for Angela Rippon in 2023. It was made of hematite mesh, with lines of silver bugle beads and strings of crystals from hemline to waist. We added silver fringe to the dress at a later date as we had to allow for Angela's incredible leg lift!'

11. Sophie Ellis-Bextor's Charleston

'I loved the playsuit, loved the gold beading and especially loved her gold shoes to match. She's like a swan, and the Charleston can be a bit erratic, but she just kept that sense of elegance the whole time, so it's a favourite of mine.'

12. AJ Odudu's Jive

'AJ was fantastic throughout the series, but I love week-one garments because it's about the celebrity's personality. They come out and it's like, "Bang, here I am!" And they embrace the show. The gold looked fantastic on her, and we could throw thousands of beads at it, so there was no holding back.'

13. Clara Amfo's Cha-cha-cha

'Clara was an absolute joy, a ray of sunshine. The ribbons on her dress had hundreds of crystals all the way up the centre of each one, so when you see it move it looks incredible. She loved it, but it also represents how hard the team worked to embellish all of those strips before attaching them to the actual base.'

14. Camilla Dallerup's Final Showdance with Tom Chambers

'Camilla was very open and allowed me to be creative with silhouette, which was great. The culotte shape – flared trousers – was a new look for us and we added embellishment around her waist and a blouse top. You might expect to see something similar on *Strictly* now, but at the time it was quite new, because people were used to seeing all the dancers in traditional ballroom dresses. So this was a turning point.'

16. Max George's Simpsons Couple's Choice

'We had to give Max some padding as well as make sure the proportions of Dianne's hair, as Marge, were right with her little dress, so that it represented the much-loved cartoon. I really love this number.'

15. Stacey Dooley's Minions *Jive*

'These numbers are fun but they're quite tricky, because when you paint someone yellow they can't lean on anybody because of transfer, and you have to go from the dress run to the live with yellow body paint everywhere. It is a logistical nightmare – we have to work hard at making something look that silly! I love it when you get people on the show who maybe didn't have themselves down for doing a *Minions* routine at the beginning but have so much fun in the process.'

17. Dev Griffin's Aladdin-*themed Couple's Choice*

'Dianne was a monkey, so we had to create texture, create fullness, which is playful with her choreography, and with Dev, there's that transfer of the blue make-up. When we have to colour people's bodies we try to create a sheath or a catsuit base, but we needed to be able to see Dev's torso, so for the hair and make-up team, that was a real challenge. Paint was coming off between the dress run and the live show – everything's being washed – but the dance was fantastic.'

18. *Amy Dowden's* Hairspray *Jive with Karim Zeroual*

'You might think Amy's dress is just blocks of black-and-white fringe, but you go from the hip area and you're reducing up to the bust area, which is a smaller circumference, so positioning the size of these blocks is a consideration. Outfits often look simple, but there's a lot of consideration about proportion, length, width, and this was one of those dresses, but it worked perfectly for their number.'

19. *Ann Widdecombe's Salsa*

'Ann Widdecombe was on the show during the previous costume designer, Su Judd's time. I love the strength of Ann, and the fact that she absolutely trusted Anton. She didn't take anything too seriously and we have lots of moments where it's elegant and stylish, but these fun moments, where people are absolutely letting go, are golden.'

20. *Ed Balls's Samba from* The Mask

'We sometimes buy a suit and reshape the shoulder line and other things, and Esra in our team bought the yellow suit for this dance. The amount of panels and the work that went into making it work for this dance is nobody's business. I loved Ed because we thought he was a serious politician, but he was really easy-going, fun and embraced it all.'

Motsi Mabuse is in a celebratory mood as she marks the twentieth birthday of *Strictly Come Dancing* and the fifth anniversary of her becoming a judge. And she promises that viewers are in for a spectacular series, with a few unexpected twists.

'I'm looking forward to surprises,' she says. 'It's 20 years of *Strictly Come Dancing*, and you might have the feeling you've seen everything, but there are always new things you haven't seen before. That's one of the reasons *Strictly* is so special. It's the combination of so many things. You have dancing, you have emotions, you have characters that you can find out more about, all the tension and the build-up. Then there's the glitz and glam. I'm excited for the whole experience, for the twists and turns, and everything this specific group can give to us.'

Motsi has been casting her eye over the new recruits and is impressed by what she has seen so far, but she's keeping any predictions to herself.

'There are some very interesting, strong characters and they are very funny,' she says. 'They got off to a great start at the launch show and I saw lots of potential. They all have the right attitude. They're serious about learning to dance but also having fun with it. I thought everybody gave an extremely good first impression, but I wouldn't pick out anyone in particular because what I've learned in five years on *Strictly* is that things can change. I give everybody a chance and we'll wait and see, but I think we're going to have one of the best series yet.'

Ahead of the new series Motsi and Head Judge Shirley have been swapping fashion ideas, and she is excited about seeing her fellow judges again, after months apart.

'I feel like in the last few years, we've grown closer, and it's fun,' she says. 'Being on the judges' panel is more about teamwork than anything, so I'm really looking forward to us getting together. Shirley and I have managed to stay in contact the whole year, which is really something beautiful, and we've got a couple of surprises of our own coming. I love expressing myself through fashion, and *Strictly* gives me the perfect platform to have fun with my looks. I can't wait for everyone to see what we've got planned!'

As the new series kicks off, Motsi still has fond memories of series 21 and the nail-biting Grand Final, which saw winner Ellie Leach battling it out with Layton Williams and Bobby Brazier.

'It was an amazing series,' she says. 'Layton gave us some real "wow" moments. Seeing how finalists Ellie, Bobby and Layton approached every dance, coming out on Saturdays and performing incredible routines – even in the early weeks, we were left thinking, "How did they manage that?" I loved Bobby's Couple's Choice, Layton's *Moulin Rouge* Paso in Musicals Week, his Argentine Tango, and Ellie's American Smooth, among many others. The Final had everything in it. There was drama, there were things that you didn't expect, quality dancing. And the viewers chose Ellie, who was a very worthy winner.'

Motsi, who was both a dancer and judge on Germany's version of *Strictly Come Dancing* before joining *Strictly* in the UK, has some advice for the new recruits.

'My advice to the new celebrities would be to keep working hard and keep the effort up,' she says. 'It's a fun show, but at the end of the day, you want to be proud of yourself, so you need to put in the work to see the results.'

While she is not picking a winner just yet, she says past champions all have one elusive quality, which clinches the Glitterball trophy. 'There's definitely something special about each winner – they all have a certain spark,' she says. 'It's a combination of passion, dedication and the ability to connect with the audience. Sometimes you can sense that spark early on, but *Strictly* is full of surprises and that's the beauty of it. The journey is as important as the destination, and sometimes the winner emerges in the most unexpected ways.'

Motsi MABUSE

While she's presented *Strictly Come Dancing* since 2010, Claudia Winkleman has been part of the *Strictly* family since becoming the first host of *It Takes Two* in 2004.

'It's amazing we've reached the 20-year mark, and it's a privilege to work on such a long-running show,' she says. 'For the viewers, *Strictly* is the run-up to Christmas, and it's so funny that every year, just as the weather turns and the leaves are turning brown, I think, "It's *Strictly* time." I think people like the show because it's multi-generational, and they can watch it with grandparents, grandchildren, their families. Plus, there's the dancing, Dave Arch and the fabulous music, and the amazing judges. It's glamorous but doesn't take itself too seriously.'

Claudia, who became the main co-host alongside Tess Daly in 2014, has seen *Strictly* evolve over two decades but says viewers can still count on the heart of the show remaining constant.

'The music has changed and we have some extra dances, but it's never completely different,' she says. 'We've still got amazing Tess, Craig and Anton, who have been there since the beginning, which is lovely because I watched every Saturday when I worked on *It Takes Two* and it's always great to see the same faces come back. I think it's stayed very close to its core, because the production team and everybody who makes it are brilliant and they know that viewers return to it again and again. I get messages from people who first started watching it when they were ten and they're still coming back to it now that they're 30 and they've got a four-year-old who wants to watch it. So it has stayed true to itself, celebrating dance and the amazing celebrities who are brave enough to give it a go.'

For all those involved in the show, the fans are of the utmost importance – Claudia says they are 'everything' to the team. 'We're so lucky that people watch and we're incredibly grateful to *Strictly* fans,' she says. 'They're so loyal. They follow the show, go to the tour, and they've got our backs. It's wonderful that it's so loved, but we won't ever take that for granted.'

Claudia was stunned by last year's Grand Final, with Ellie Leach, Bobby Brazier and Layton Williams all fighting for first place.

'It was extraordinary,' she says. 'Ellie and Vito were unbelievable, a very good combination. But the whole group were brilliant last year. Every year, I think nobody can be as good as that and somehow it happens again.'

As the corks pop for the twentieth anniversary, Claudia is excited about the latest line-up of celebrities eager to take to the dance floor. 'The launch show was amazing. They are an excellent bunch,' she says. 'They're really fun and we had a great laugh. They're super bouncy and they are all up for it. There's a great camaraderie and they're hilarious with each other already. I think each one is completely brilliant and I'm excited about 2024.

'Also, it was lovely to have Amy back because she really wanted that, and we missed her so much. And we missed Aljaž after his two-year break.'

Ahead of the live shows, Claudia is looking forward to being reunited with the judges and to watching the couples take to the floor for the first time.

'The first dance is completely thrilling because they're nervous and, even if you watch rehearsal footage, you have no idea what it's going to be like when there's a live audience and everybody comes out. So I can't wait to see them dance.

'What I love about *Strictly*, especially at the beginning, is that there are so many dances, so there will be comedy, there will be romantic dances, there will be drama with a Paso Doble. Even if you think one dance isn't for you, three minutes later, you get another one!'

Claudia WINKLEMAN

Jamie BORTHWICK

EastEnders star Jamie has already had a brief taste of *Strictly* glory, having won the 2023 Christmas special with Nancy Xu, scoring a perfect 40 for his Quickstep. It was an experience that left him hungry for more.

'I wouldn't say it was a head start,' he says. 'I'm all right on the Quickstep, but that was just one dance. Learning a different ballroom and Latin dance each week is a whole other kettle of fish, as well as the public having their say. But I loved doing the Christmas show. I loved being in the environment. I loved being with the gang, so when they asked me to do the series it was a no-brainer. I couldn't wait to go back and be with everyone and meet some new pals along the way.'

Londoner Jamie was just 12 when he landed the part of Jay Brown in *EastEnders*, in 2006. He is now one of the longest-serving actors on the BBC soap. The role earned him a 2008 British Soap Award for Best Dramatic Performance from a Young Actor, and he bagged Best Actor at the Inside Soap Awards in 2023.

Jamie is paired with Michelle Tsiakkas and says she will 'have to have patience, know how to have a laugh – and incorporate naps in the rehearsal room'. She will also need to spend some time on the Albert Square set, as Jamie will still be filming between training sessions.

'I'm still doing *EastEnders* as normal, so I've just budgeted for that, knowing that I'll be really busy for the next however long I'm in the show,' he says. 'I'm in for a penny, in for a pound. I like to be busy. I'll just take each day as it comes.'

With a packed schedule ahead, the actor is at the peak of his fitness, after training for the 2024 marathon earlier this year. 'I've kept up my fitness a little bit, so I'm hoping I've still got some marathon training in reserve.'

While Jamie is happy to don the Lycra Latin outfits and plenty of sparkle, he has drawn the line at one *Strictly* staple.

'I'm happy to wear the bolero jackets and open-necked shirts, but I'm not going to have a fake tan!'

Having faced the judges before, with brilliant results, Jamie is not expecting to see the rare 10 paddles coming up every week, and he's ready to take any feedback on the chin.

'I can't wait for the judges' comments – bring it on!'

In her third year on *Strictly Come Dancing*, Michelle is excited to be dancing with her first celebrity partner, *EastEnders* star Jamie Borthwick.

'I love teaching and I've been waiting for this moment to get the full *Strictly* experience,' she says. 'It is an amazing feeling to be able to be creative and work with a celebrity and teach. It's really exciting. I feel very lucky that I was given Jamie, because not only is he talented and a hard worker, but he's also a lovely person and we get along really well. Our practice sessions are hard work mixed with laughter and a lot of banter. It's the perfect balance.'

A keen pupil, Jamie is responding well to Michelle's teaching and she says the pair are relaxed in each other's company.

'We can be really natural around each other and just be ourselves,' she says. 'Jamie doesn't take anything too seriously, which is great because he always says to me, "Just tell me straight." I'm quite direct, but I think since we've both got that same trait we work well together. He's a lot of fun and we laugh a lot, which is important.'

Michelle began competing at the age of six in her native Cyprus and was Cypriot National Champion for 10 consecutive years. She studied architecture at the University of Kent, in Canterbury, before returning to dance full-time at 19. She joined the *Strictly* professional team in 2022.

With Jamie having won the Christmas special – with a Quickstep that scored 40 – Michelle says there's a lot to live up to.

'Jamie's set the bar high for himself, which puts a bit of pressure on him, but each dance is completely different,' she says. 'When you start with a new dance, you're practically starting from scratch. It will be difficult for him as people may have high expectations, but I think he's got a good mentality and we share the same attitude, that all you can do is your best. We're going to work hard, have fun and enjoy the moment.'

Although he kicked off the series with a Viennese Waltz, Michelle says Jamie is looking forward to showing his Latin moves.

'I've tried to introduce him slowly to a lot of different dances, and he's told me that he prefers Latin,' she says. 'I think he will be good at both. People have seen the Quickstep, but I think he's got the Latin flair, so I've got high hopes for the Latin as well.'

Going into the live shows and preparing for her first couple dances, Michelle is also facing the judges for the first time – but she says Jamie has a good approach to the comments ahead.

'It's a competition but we're also here to learn, so we will take on all the judges' remarks and use them to improve,' she says. 'Jamie's the same; he wants the full *Strictly* experience. I think he'll be fine.'

'Jamie is filming *EastEnders* in Elstree, close to where we are rehearsing, so we are fitting training round his work,' says Michelle. 'So I hope to get a tour of Albert Square!'

Michelle TSIAKKAS

Pete WICKS

Reality star and podcaster Pete Wicks might be a frequent face in Essex's nightclubs, but he claims he's no natural when it comes to dancing – and usually heads in the opposite direction to the dance floor when the banging tunes come on.

'Dancing is so far out of my comfort zone, and when my friends are on the floor, I'm at the bar,' he says. 'But *Strictly* is a once-in-a-lifetime opportunity. This is actually the show I always said I wouldn't do, and dancing live in front of the nation every Saturday is absolutely terrifying, but that's part of the reason I am doing it. This is going to be the biggest challenge for me, but I'm so excited about doing it. I'm starting from a solid zero and that's the most exciting part, because it's a blank canvas. We'll see what happens. It could be a masterpiece. I imagine it won't be, but we'll see. I'm genuinely looking forward to getting stuck in.'

Essex boy Pete was born in Harlow and joined the cast of *The Only Way Is Essex* (*TOWIE*) in the fifteenth series, in 2015. Since then, he has carved out a TV career, appearing on *Celebrity Island with Bear Grylls*, *Celebrity MasterChef* and *The Real Full Monty* as well as presenting on the red carpet at the BRIT Awards, Pride of Britain Awards and National Television Awards. Along with best friend Sam Thompson, he also presents the award-nominated podcast *Staying Relevant*, which has over 5 million downloads to date and has reached number one in the comedy charts.

While Pete, who is paired with former champion Jowita Przystał, is a self-confessed dance novice, it's not the ballroom steps that are keeping him awake at night – but another kind.

'It's weird, but my biggest fear is going up the stairs to the Clauditorium,' he says. 'After I've done a dance, I'll be so tired. Have you seen the pace the couples all run up those stairs?

'Also, a big fear for me is not getting the opportunity to fulfil my potential. I want to do as well as I can, I want to learn something new. I'm really enjoying it and it's such a fun thing to do, plus it's a wonderful skill that you can take with you for the rest of your life. I want to get as much out of it as possible.'

Known for some explosive scenes in *TOWIE*, Pete promises to bring some of that drama to the dance floor.

'On screen, I've been lucky enough to make a living from just being myself, so I'll do the same with dancing,' he says. 'It'll be as me, whether that means bringing the fire or not. And it probably will.'

The stylish star is gearing up for a change of image for the ballroom and embracing the sparkle. 'I notoriously love black, which is probably off the table for the most part, so I've decided that I'm "In for a Penny, in for a Pound Pete",' he says. 'I've told the costume team they can be as wild as they possibly want …!'

Former *Strictly Come Dancing* champ Jowita Przystał is hoping to add a second Glitterball trophy to her mantelpiece in her third year on the show, and is thrilled to be dancing with *TOWIE* star Pete Wicks.

'I'm over the moon,' she says. 'The moment we met we clicked, and I love his sense of humour. I cannot stop laughing when I'm with him.

'The first thing he said when we were paired was, "Oh, it's not Johannes!"' which made me laugh so that's a good sign that I get his jokes! It's really important that he feels comfortable with the person he's paired up with. We work very well together.'

While Pete admits he is starting from scratch, Jowita says he has the right attitude and may have hidden talents.

'I believe he can dance even if he thinks he can't,' she says. 'I will make him a dancer. He's willing to work hard, he's absolutely dedicated and he's a very good student, so I'm really positive.'

Her new pupil impressed her in the first group dance, and Jowita says he's already showcased his 'signature move'. 'Sometimes people get stressed about being on camera, dancing for the first time, but he is the opposite. He's a real performer, which is a good thing, but also he adds his own twist to everything, so he might surprise me and do a completely different routine than the one we rehearsed. But we'll go with the flow!'

Jowita also thinks Pete might surprise the audience with the more elegant dances. 'Everyone thinks he will be more Latin, but I see a bit of a ballroom boy in him,' she says.

Born in Poland, Jowita began dancing at six and went on to become Polish Open Latin Champion.

She won *The Greatest Dancer* and performed on *Strictly* for the first time in 2020. She joined the show as a professional dancer the following year, then won the Glitterball trophy in 2022 with TV wildlife presenter Hamza Yassin. In 2023, she partnered Paralympic cyclist Jody Cundy – who picked up his sixth gold medal in Paris this summer.

'It was amazing partnering Jody and I'm so proud of him,' she says. 'Getting that gold medal is a huge achievement. I know how hard he works and how dedicated he is to his discipline. I learned so much from him, and I felt honoured to be with such a champion.'

Jowita's favourite dance with Jody was their emotional American Smooth to the music from Pixar's *Up* in Movie Week.

'It was magical,' says Jowita.

As *Strictly* turns 20, Jowita says she is 'speechless' to be part of a show that celebrates 'pure love for dancing'.

'The show is so magical,' she says. 'All of us love dance and want to share that passion. The people who work on the show are all at the top of their game and all love *Strictly*, which is what I think the audience can feel and connect with at home. Now we are celebrating the twentieth anniversary, I feel honoured to be part of such a massive show, and I'm looking forward to being back in the studio to create more magic.'

Jowita PRZYSTAŁ

When the now-famous *Strictly* theme tune rang out for the first time and Tess stepped out onto the studio floor, in 2004, she couldn't have known she would still be there today, celebrating two decades of success.

'It's hard to believe that it's been 20 years of *Strictly* because I remember the first show as though it was last year,' she says. 'It was a huge deal for me, working alongside Sir Bruce Forsyth, who I'd grown up watching on TV, and to be standing by his side on a studio floor was truly a pinch-yourself moment. Bruce was a gentleman and taught me so much about television.

'The show was experimental. We had no idea it would capture the nation's imagination and become the juggernaut it did, turning into a global smash hit with versions in over 50 countries.

'Working on *Strictly* has always been an honour, simply because it brings joy to so many people. You feel part of something special that people look forward to every year. It is warm, it's joyful, celebratory in tone – and that, in itself, is a gift.'

Since the first show, which saw eight couples compete, Tess has seen *Strictly* evolve while always staying true to its roots.

'The most dramatic change is probably Craig's hairstyle!' she jokes. 'I love the long hair and beard. But, seriously, we've moved on a lot. When we started, we had one burgundy velvet curtain behind the judges and a few fairy lights. Now the lighting is breathtaking, along with the other incredible effects. It seems to go up another notch every year. We now have wonderful theme weeks that viewers love, whether it's movies, musicals or Halloween. They've grown to become standout shows on their own.

'Viewers become invested with the celebrities and warm to them as people as we go with them on their journey. Annabel Croft was a wonderful example, because she wore her heart on her sleeve and shared her grief at losing her beloved husband. That touched so many of us. We warm to the human stories and grow to care. That's part of the magic, because you're watching someone work hard towards a common goal and you're with them for that emotional ride.'

Along with the personal stories, this year Tess thinks we're in for a lot of laughs. 'I don't think we've ever come across such a collectively exuberant group as this batch of celebrities,' she says. 'At the launch show, their energy was bouncing off the walls and there was so much banter, it was a laugh a minute. They all have bags of personality, and Claudia and I couldn't get a word in edgeways, they had so much to say. Let's hope their feet can also do the talking.'

While Tess can't wait for the class of 2024 to take to the dance floor, she says series 21 was one to beat.

'Last year was brilliant because you couldn't call an early winner. It was anyone's race and it was nail-biting right to the last moment, which makes for a great Final.'

As we go into the live shows, our *Strictly* host is as excited as ever for the series ahead. 'This year we have a new theme, Icons Week, which I'm really looking forward to,' she says. 'I always love the first live show, because it's thrilling to watch their first dance in front of the live audience. It's bound to be nerve-racking and my heart goes out to them, so I want to hold their hands through that process, but it's unmissable television.'

Tess is also delighted to welcome back two familiar faces this year. 'I am so thrilled to have Amy back where she belongs. She was beaming with delight throughout the launch show, and she told us it has given her a huge boost being back, because she really missed it.

'I've also missed Aljaž. He's loads of fun so it's wonderful to see him back on the dance floor.'

In her role as host, Tess often talks to fans about their love of *Strictly* and is proud of how the show brings families together.

'Families sitting in the same room watching TV on Saturday nights is becoming increasingly rare, and I think it's special for that reason,' she says. 'Viewers tell us they plan their Saturday nights around it. They might get a takeaway, invite extended family or have friends for viewing parties. It's became a part of people's autumn schedule and they tell us they don't mind the onset of winter because *Strictly* is coming back. There is so much warmth towards the show, and that means so much. Being a part of that is a privilege.'

Tess DALY

Montell DOUGLAS

She's known as Fire on *Gladiators*, and Montell Douglas will be hoping to set the dance floor alight on this year's show.

'I've been waiting for this my whole life,' she says. 'I was like, Olympic Games, tick, *Gladiators*, tick. *Strictly* was next on the list. I've always wanted to do the show. I think it will bring out elements of me that I don't show very often. This is so fa*r in* my comfort zone, to be able to fully express yourself. I'm all about that, and I haven't been able to do that with many of the things I've done before. There was no way I was going to say no!'

In 2010, Montell won Commonwealth Gold in the 4-by-100-metre relay race, and also held the British women's record for the fastest 100-metre sprint. In 2022, she became the first British woman to compete in both the summer and winter Olympics, as part of the two-woman bobsleigh team representing Great Britain at the Beijing Winter Olympics, 14 years after running in the athletics at the summer games in the same city. In May 2023, it was announced that Montell would join the *Gladiators* reboot as Fire.

Although she has no dance training, the sports star is no shrinking violet when it comes to strutting her stuff at a party.

'I'm the first person on the dance floor, last to leave,' she says. 'I'll do it all, it doesn't matter what's on the turntable. I absolutely love dance. I don't know about the skill level, but I've got natural rhythm, for sure.

'I have always used dance and music in my training, so when I'm competing for a championship or any race, I've got headphones on and I'm dancing. When I was a sprinter, it used to distract me from performing on the big stage for the 100 metres and it helped relax me. I have no idea how I'm going to prepare for the actual dances, because I can't dance to distract me from the dance!'

Montell, who is paired with Johannes Radebe for the show, says one of her biggest challenges will be in the footwear department.

'I'm nervous about the heels,' she says. 'I'm five foot ten inches, and six foot plus in heels. I'm a casual girl, sports kit every day, and I live in trainers.'

The London-born star is already a familiar face to Saturday-night viewers and she is looking to bring her warrior mentality to ballroom.

'I am so honoured to have been asked to do the show,' she says. 'It is such an amazing thing to be a part of and I can't wait to get started. Hopefully, a few of my *Gladiators* moves will come in handy with the Tango or Paso Doble!'

This year, Johannes Radebe will be burning up the floor with Gladiator Montell Douglas – also known as 'Fire' – and he's ready to sizzle.

'Every partner is a surprise,' he says. 'I'm so happy because Montell is a joy to be with, and the first thing that she said to me was, "Can we please just laugh and enjoy the experience?" The fact that she likes to laugh at herself and make me laugh means rehearsals so far have been really chilled and so much fun. But at the same time, she's an athlete and she takes me through my paces with her stamina.'

As an Olympian and a star of TV's *Gladiators*, Montell certainly has fighting spirit, and Johannes says she is also a huge fan of *Strictly*.

'With my partners, I am always caring and encouraging, but Montell is encouraging me – and she is so excited,' he says. 'She said, "I didn't ever think that this would happen to me," and I know that feeling, because it reminded me of my first time on *Strictly*. She approaches this whole experience with gratitude, which always makes my heart sing. You want a partner who's going to commit themselves and already she says she is waking up thinking of steps and counting, which is fabulous.'

As a sportswoman, Montell is supremely fit, but in the training room she is having to focus on the details of dance.

'Dancing is a whole different ballgame,' he says. 'The detail in everything has taken her by surprise. For example, in running she was told, "Don't turn out your feet," and I'm telling her to do the opposite, so that has been a challenge for her.'

'Also, on *Gladiators* she steps into a character, which is fantastic for the many different dances and the acting skills needed to perform them.'

Born in Zamdela, South Africa, Johannes began dancing at seven and is two-time Professional South African Latin Champion and three-time South African Amateur Latin Champion. He joined the South African version of *Strictly Come Dancing* in 2014 before moving to the UK show six years ago. He reached the Grand Final in 2021 with John Whaite and last year made the semi-final with tennis legend Annabel Croft – but says their friendship meant more than the Glitterball trophy.

'Annabel and her family have become family to me, and that's the gift that *Strictly Come Dancing* has brought to me,' he says. 'My life is richer with Annabel in it. She reminded me that life is for living.'

The couple performed an emotional Couple's Choice, and Johannes says that was a special moment.

'It was a beautiful tribute to her husband,' he says. 'It was such a special dance for us.'

Johannes is celebrating 10 years since he joined the South African version of the show, as well as *Strictly*'s twentieth birthday.

'I'm honoured to be a part of this,' he says. '*Strictly* is the gift that keeps on giving, not only to us and everyone that works here. It brings so much joy to so many people.

'There are no words to describe the feeling when we went back this year – like every year. That first day in the studio when we hear the band play and the lights are on, it's a real buzz. The show has changed my life, and I feel honoured to be a part of such a milestone.'

Johannes RADEBE

Chris McCAUSLAND

unny man Chris is hoping to bring his unique brand of humour to *Strictly Come Dancing*, and is the first blind contestant on the show. But asked about his dance experience, he jokes, 'I had to practise walking down the stairs eight times. If I have to do that eight times, how am I going to dance on live TV?

'If anybody out there is thinking, "How is he going to do that?" then rest assured that I am thinking exactly the same thing. I don't dance, I can't dance and I can't see the dancing I will have to do. What can possibly go wrong? Okay, don't answer that ...!'

For the last 20 years, the Liverpudlian comedian has been a TV regular on shows like *Have I Got News for You*, *Would I Lie to You?*, *QI*, *The Last Leg* and *8 out of 10 Cats Does Countdown*. He has also appeared on *Live at the Apollo* three times, hosting in 2021, and the same year he made his debut appearance at the Royal Variety Performance. He also presents the ITV Saturday-morning chat show *The Chris McCausland Show*, and has co-written and starred in the festive film *Bad Tidings*, which is set to premiere this Christmas.

Chris and his *Strictly* partner, two-time finalist Dianne Buswell, are determined to overcome any obstacles.

'We decided we'd just figure it out as we go along,' he says. 'Everyone on the show has been really nice and supportive. I've never watched the show, for obvious reasons, so I don't really know what the dances entail. They're being very flexible and Dianne is figuring out how to teach me as we go. It's a work in progress.'

Having taken part in the launch-show group dance, Chris does admit to a few aching muscles after the initial training.

'It's been pretty tiring to be honest,' he laughs. 'I can't believe that this is the beginning. I can only imagine that over time you get used to it. It's been loads of fun but there's a huge period of concentration that you need to get past, when you are trying to remember the moves, before you can even start to smile. On the first day I did six hours, but I was smiling at the end.'

The stand-up comic, usually seen in a smart shirt on stage, is ready to fully embrace his *Strictly* wardrobe – as well as having the first spray tan of his life.

'I've had some time to acclimatise my mind to it,' he says. 'Again, it's an unknown to me, so until someone hands me something and tells me to put it on, I don't know what the costumes are like that we'll be wearing in the show. I've decided to wear what I'm told and get the fake tan straight away. For me, the biggest fear was not being able to leave those inhibitions at the door, so I intend to go for it.'

Before being paired with comedian Chris McCausland, Dianne Buswell was already a huge fan, and she's delighted he's chosen to take to the dance floor. As Strictly's first blind contestant, Chris is breaking new ground on the show.

'I was excited to be partnered with Chris because I really wanted to dance with him,' she says. 'I've known about Chris for a long time and I've watched his comedy. I think he's hilarious. I welcomed the challenge because I know this is something that has never been done before, but if it's done right, it's going to be amazing.'

'We are already having so much fun. Chris is such a hard worker. He just keeps on going and going. He wants to push himself and enjoy the whole experience.'

Dianne, a seasoned tutor, who has been part of Strictly since 2017, is on her own learning curve as she teaches Chris to master dance steps.

'I didn't realise how much you rely on visuals when showing somebody dance moves,' she says. 'It's a big part of how we teach. For example, as well as showing steps, if someone is struggling, I could show them a video of what a Cha-cha-cha looks like. With Chris, I have to be more descriptive, trying to think of things that I can compare moves to so there's a picture in his head. His pathway to success is going to be unique, so both Chris and I are working it out as we go.'

Dianne is impressed by Chris's ear for music and natural rhythm, and says: 'His musicality is brilliant. Once he knows the song in his head and he knows what steps go to that song, he's fantastic, so that is his strong point. He's also enjoying the chance to do something physical and get fit.

'Chris's sense of humour is so dry that he plays things down a lot, but secretly, I know he's loving this process.'

Born in Bunbury, Australia, Dianne danced with brother Andrew from a young age and became Australian Open Champion and four-time Amateur Australian Open Finalist. After a year on Dancing with the Stars in her homeland, she moved to Strictly for series 15, dancing with the Reverend Richard Coles. A year later, she reached the Grand Final with social-media star Joe Sugg, and last year she repeated the feat with actor Bobby Brazier.

'Bobby has a special place in my heart,' she says. 'He was brilliant, a lot of fun, and I couldn't have asked for a better partner. He did ask for daily naps, despite being only 20, and Chris hasn't asked for one of those yet! But Bobby was a quick learner and an amazing dancer.'

The couple danced many beautiful routines on the way to the Final, but Dianne remembers two as particularly special.

'My favourite dance was our Couple's Choice, dedicated to Bobby's mum, Jade, because it had so much meaning and it really was a lovely moment for both of us,' she says. 'But I also loved our Quickstep, because Bobby was so good at ballroom.'

As well as being the twentieth anniversary of Strictly, this series holds a special significance for Dianne, as close pal Amy Dowden was welcomed back in a group dance, after a year off battling illness.

'It's so exciting having Amy back,' she says. 'Her family were in the audience for the launch show and I was so happy for all of them. It was a beautiful moment and I couldn't wipe the smile off my face.'

Dianne BUSWELL

Janette returns to *It Takes Two* this year and will once again share hosting duties with Fleur East, who made her debut as presenter last year.

'It will be incredible to work with Fleur again,' she says. 'I love Fleur and we're so similar as people. It's wonderful to work with somebody you get on with so well.'

As a former professional on the show, Janette thinks her co-host's experience as a contestant and finalist, in series 20, makes her the perfect companion as a host.

'Fleur is a natural in front of the camera,' she says. 'Also, because she was a celebrity on the show, got all the way to the Final and did the *Strictly Come Dancing* Live Tour, she has been there and walked in their shoes, so she knows exactly how the celebrities are feeling.'

Janette, who danced with a celebrity partner on the show for eight series, from 2013, is excited to meet the latest line-up of stars heading for the dance floor – and the *It Takes Two* sofa.

'Every year, the celebrity line-up surprises us with their talent,' she says. 'I eagerly await seeing what they bring to the table and, as this is the twentieth anniversary, I'm sure it will be filled with so much magic, once again.'

She's also delighted that husband Aljaž Škorjanec, with whom she shares daughter Lyra, will be back on the *Strictly Come Dancing* dance floor after a two-year absence.

'Aljaž is absolutely buzzing to be back and the UK gets to enjoy the smiliest man in showbiz once again!'

Catching up with the competing couples is one of Janette's favourite things about *It Takes Two*, and she says the series 21 alumni were fabulous both on and off the dance floor.

'It was such a great series, with a little bit of everything. Having Angela Rippon, that legend of British television and former presenter of *Come Dancing*, joining our show was incredible, and on top of that, at 79, she showed the world it doesn't really matter how old you are; you can dance. *Strictly* always has something for everyone, but I think that was true of last year more than ever. I loved the Final. Any of those finalists could have been the winners and every one of them was beautiful to watch, but Ellie pushing herself, trusting Vito and doing this complex choreography. It was amazing.

'I was there the day of the final rehearsal so I got to watch all the showdances before they performed them on the Saturday. Then I watched Ellie and Vito's showdance and I almost cried because she was somebody who'd never danced before, who, after 15 weeks, delivered that routine! The perseverance, the determination and the self-belief that Ellie and Vito had was beautiful to see.'

As presenter of the *Strictly Come Dancing* Live Tour Janette gets to see some of the fan favourites danced again, night after night. 'I loved the Live Tour,' she says. 'There were many great moments. I felt like I was watching a real West End performance. Also, the professional dancers did some epic group numbers, including the Barbie-inspired dance. You should have seen the kids' faces in the arenas every time that routine came on with Dianne in her Barbie-inspired outfit and everybody dressed as their own interpretations of Barbie or Ken. It was such a fun tour.'

As a former professional dancer on the show, Janette loves to watch the professional group numbers every week.

'I love everything about the show, but when the professional dancers come together for those numbers, I really look forward to watching them do what they do, at their absolute best. I can't wait to see the incredible professional group dances on the *Strictly Come Dancing* dance floor this year.'

Take 20

Almost 300 contestants have danced on the main series of *Strictly Come Dancing* in the two decades since it launched in 2004, and 21 winners have been crowned. But how well do you remember our *Strictly* stars?

On these pages are clues to 20 of the finalists from the last 20 years, both celebrity contestants and professionals.

Can you name each person and match them to their picture?

1. He came from a fictional farm, won the Glitterball trophy and went on to front his own TV show about a real farm.

2. Born in Ptuj, Slovenia, this professional danced to victory with Abbey Clancy in series 11.

3. He went from sitting on the BBC Breakfast sofa to Singin' in the Rain and Strictly champ.

4. The first male celebrity to win, this fast bowler played cricket for Yorkshire for 15 years and England for 11 years.

5. This professional dancer hails from South Africa and has lifted the Glitterball trophy twice.

6. More used to sitting behind a news desk, she proved a whizz on the dance floor and became the first ever Strictly champ.

7. This England rugby player made it to the Final in series four before losing the crown to a cricketer.

8. This dancer became the first professional to lift the Glitterball trophy twice, first in 2011 and again in 2015.

9. The only Olympian to have clinched the Strictly title, he also danced the first barefoot showdance.

10. A professional on the show since 2016, she has danced with a former Chancellor of the Exchequer, two Olympic athletes and a footballer among others. She claimed the Glitterball trophy with an actor.

D

O

K

11. Olympic heptathlete who won gold at the Sydney games in 2000, before reaching the Final of series two and losing out to Jill Halfpenny.

12. A comedian, psychologist and author who starred in *Not the Nine O'Clock News* before reaching the Strictly Final in series eight.

13. A finalist in series three, this talented presenter went on to host *It Takes Two* for 10 years.

14. The first of two Holby City actors to wear the Strictly crown, winning series six — nine years before castmate Joe McFadden.

15. Boyband drummer who proved he had skin in the game by lifting the series-nine trophy.

R

B

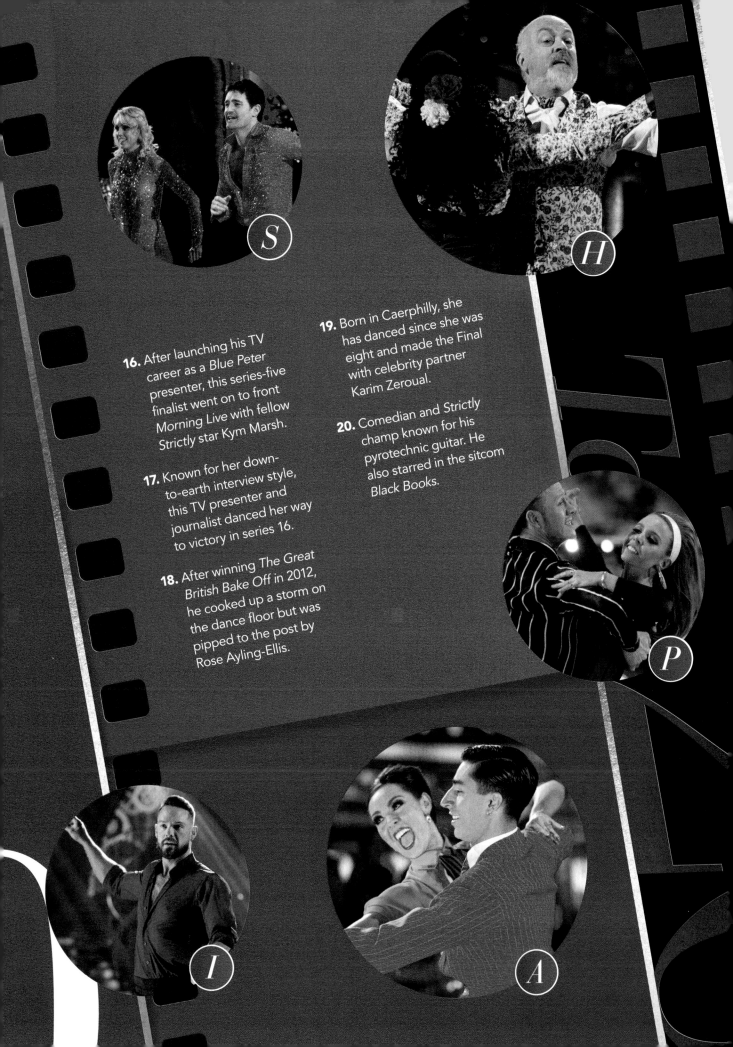

S

H

16. After launching his TV career as a Blue Peter presenter, this series-five finalist went on to front Morning Live with fellow Strictly star Kym Marsh.

17. Known for her down-to-earth interview style, this TV presenter and journalist danced her way to victory in series 16.

18. After winning The Great British Bake Off in 2012, he cooked up a storm on the dance floor but was pipped to the post by Rose Ayling-Ellis.

19. Born in Caerphilly, she has danced since she was eight and made the Final with celebrity partner Karim Zeroual.

20. Comedian and Strictly champ known for his pyrotechnic guitar. He also starred in the sitcom Black Books.

P

I

A

Toyah WILCOX

It's no 'mystery' why rock legend Toyah Willcox has signed up for *Strictly Come Dancing* – she's been a fan of the show for two decades.

'I've always wanted to do *Strictly*,' she says. 'I love the idea of dancing. I think dancing is one of the most extraordinary things about being a human being. I think it's the greatest way of expressing and getting in touch with your emotions. Music has always made me want to dance, so it feels very natural to have said yes to *Strictly*.'

Born in Birmingham, Toyah began her career as an actress, starring in the BBC play *Glitter*, the subversive Derek Jarman film *Jubilee* and cult classic *Quadrophenia*, before becoming a punk-rock legend with a string of hit singles, including 'It's a Mystery', 'I Want to Be Free' and 'Brave New World'. Over a 50-year career, she has had 13 top-40 singles, recorded 25 albums, written two books and acted in over 40 stage plays and over 20 films, as well as presented numerous TV shows. Married to rock guitarist Robert Fripp, the pair brightened up lockdown with their online videos *Toyah & Robert's Sunday Lunch*, and earlier this year they played together at Glastonbury.

While she has a musical background, Toyah says the style of ballroom and Latin music is a far cry from the tracks of her trade.

'I think my musical experience is helping. I hear and read music, which hopefully makes a big difference.'

Even so, she hasn't ruled out dancing to one of her own songs in the show.

'I was in a crossover period from the late seventies into the eighties, so I went from high-energy punk into almost ploddy rock,' she says.

The singer-songwriter usually keeps fit with gym sessions, but she admits that training for *Strictly* has taken her exertion levels up a notch.

'We're going full-on, but it's exhilarating and so beautiful. The team and everyone on the show are so encouraging.'

When the going gets tough, Toyah will be taking inspiration from an unlikely *Strictly* hero. 'I loved Ann Widdecombe on the show,' she says. 'I loved her strength of personality, her conviction, her self-confidence. That's a real focus point for me. If I'm feeling I can't do something, I'll just channel my inner Ann Widdecombe.'

With a lifetime of stage experience, Toyah, who is dancing with Neil Jones, is ready to face the judges' comments and promises to stay positive.

'I view the judges as being more for the audience at home than for us,' she says. 'So I'll keep smiling and not answer back.'

Having worn some outlandish costumes throughout her punk days and in her many stage personas, the star is also embracing the glitter and glam of the *Strictly* makeover.

'The costumes are so clever, so beautiful. They really know how to mould you and make you look your best. It's exhilarating. The dress goes on and I think, "Wow!"'

Paired with singer and actress Toyah Willcox, dancer Neil Jones is getting creative and planning some unforgettable routines.

'My motto is, let's just entertain people,' he says. 'I love teaching someone how to dance. Toyah is a singer – she's so musical, so when you put on the music, she gets the feeling, she understands how it flows, which is really helpful. She's brilliant. She has so much energy and she's so focused. We are getting on so well and she's the perfect student.'

In the fortnight before the first live show, Neil put Toyah through her paces, trying out different styles of dance, before teaching her steps for their debut Tango. Her dedication from the start of the process made a big impression on him.

'The first day I started teaching her the actual routine she asked if she could video me going through it, so she filmed me doing the steps slowly. Then, after a full day's rehearsal, she went home and practised. The following day she had memorised everything we'd gone over, which is brilliant. She's got so much energy and she's giving it everything.'

After taking her through the initial paces, Neil thinks rocker Toyah is going to be an all-rounder on the dance floor.

'I actually think her ability is the same in both ballroom and Latin, which is really good,' he says. 'She wants to give it everything.'

Neil was born in Münster, Germany, where his army dad was stationed, and began dancing at age three. He has represented Finland, the Netherlands and the UK, and holds 45 dance championship titles, including eight-time British National, eight-time Dutch National, European and four-time World Latin Champion. He joined the *Strictly Come Dancing* professional team in 2016 and has previously partnered footballer Alex Scott and comedian Nina Wadia.

As one of the longest-serving professionals on *Strictly Come Dancing*, he is still struck by the love the fans have for the programme.

'The show is still going strong and winning awards,' he says. 'I think *Strictly* evolves but the heart of it stays the same. It's still that show that we've grown to love from the beginning, yet it is still able to push boundaries.

'At this year's National Television Awards we could feel the support from everyone that loves *Strictly*, and this year the cast is stronger than ever. I've never laughed so much in my life as I did at the launch show. The celebrities this year are brilliant. Just being around them, you can see they're going to be really entertaining. It's going to be a good year.'

Neil JONES

JB GILL

Popstar and farmer JB Gill is swapping his wellies for Waltzes and is looking forward to glamming up. 'I walked into wardrobe earlier and they said I was such a dream,' he laughs. 'I was saying yes to the coral shirt, yes to the yellow trousers, whatever you want. From the fields of my farm to sequins and glitter – I'm here to embrace it all!'

JB shot to fame as part of JLS, the *X Factor* finalists who went on to become one of the UK's biggest boybands, with five number-one singles and over 10 million record sales worldwide. He is also an award-winning farmer as well as educating the nation about life in the country on CBeebies' *Down on the Farm* and Channel 5's *On the Farm*. He is a regular presenter on BBC *Songs of Praise* and hosts the TV show *Cooking with the Gills* with wife Chloe.

JB has had a brief taste of the *Strictly* process after performing a Jive on the Christmas special in 2012. 'I loved the Christmas special, and I've been keen to get back to the floor, but the end of the year for me is always quite busy because I'm often on tour with the boys,' he says. 'This is the first year that the dates have aligned and everything worked itself out, so I had to say yes. I'm raring to go and looking forward to showing off some new skills to the JLS boys.'

JB is following in the footsteps of bandmate Aston Merrygold, who competed in series 15, and couldn't wait to tell his pal he has signed up.

'I called him on FaceTime, and I was sitting with my wife and as soon as he saw us he said, "Oh, gosh!" I said, "No, listen. It's not a baby!" The first thing he thought was that Gill baby number three was on its way. As soon as I said it was *Strictly*, he was very excited. I came to watch him when he was in it, so he'll definitely be at the live shows.'

Between gigs and tough manual labour on the farm, JB should have plenty of stamina for the rehearsals – and partner Amy Dowden has already given him a pep talk to get him in the right frame of mind for the competition ahead.

'It's thrilling, it's so exciting. Amy and I have established a connection and we're in it together. Amy told me, "It's up to you. You're only in competition with yourself. At the end of the day, you want to improve on the things you did last week and keep improving, and you want to have the most fun you can."'

Welsh professional Amy Dowden is making an emotional return to the *Strictly* dance floor after a brave battle with cancer. Her fellow professionals marked her welcome return with a special group dance in the launch show, and she says it was a huge moment for her.

'It's just wonderful to be back,' she says. 'When I was back on the dance floor with all the dancers, that's the moment I felt like myself again. I've been doing all the rehab, the physio, everything I possibly could to get fit again, but actually it wasn't until I was back with the gang, doing what I love most, that I truly felt like me again.

'The launch-show dance was lovely,' she says. 'My friends and family were there, my husband Ben was there, and it was super emotional but also one big celebration of me coming through everything. I'm so honoured, blessed and lucky that this *Strictly* family supported me throughout everything that I went through.'

Born and raised in Caerphilly, Amy took up dancing at eight and she and partner Ben Jones became British Open Latin Dance Champions in 2017, the first all-British pair to take the title in over 30 years. Amy is also four-time British National Finalist and a British National Champion. She joined *Strictly* in 2017, dancing with Brian Conley, and two years later reached the Grand Final with Karim Zeroual. This year, she is paired with JLS star JB Gill and says she wants him to 'make memories for a lifetime, fall in love with ballroom dancing and make him and his family proud'. She adds:

'JB is so lovely and he's got so much potential. Being in a band means his strengths are musicality and natural rhythm. He's still learning the fundamentals, which, for everyone, takes time. But he picks up the routines super fast.

'What I love most is that he's so invested in it and he wants to do it properly. He wants to know the technique, the fundamentals, and he's so hard-working. He's also so smiley and positive. He's the perfect partner for my comeback, so I'm really grateful.'

JLS fans may think JB would lean towards the Latin dances, but Amy believes he has some surprises up his sleeve.

'Our first dance was a Waltz and he really surprised me,' she says. 'There's so much elegance. I really thought he was going to be a Latin boy, but I think he will surprise everyone and be a ballroom boy.'

Amy was already a dancer when *Strictly* first aired, 20 years ago, and she was instantly a fan.

'I remember it was my dream to one day become a *Strictly* professional. I have to pinch myself every year that I'm back on this show, and it still feels like I'm living in one big dream.

'It's a show that gives so much pleasure. It is our escape from winter, the build-up to Christmas with the beautiful costumes, the music, the lights. I saw it for myself last year when I was on the oncology unit and everyone was talking about it. I felt so proud to be part of this show.'

As well as being reunited with her *Strictly* family, Amy is delighted that Aljaž is back in the team. 'I keep saying the two As are back. Aljaž brings such warmth, such energy, and he's so endearing, so it's fabulous. Perfect for the twentieth year.

'It feels like my first year again, after everything I went through last year. It's great to have a partner, because teaching is my passion and I'm so excited about everything, from the live shows to trying on costumes, to Blackpool and all the speciality weeks. I'm going to make the most of everything.'

Amy **DOWDEN MBE**

With 20 years under his sparkly *Strictly* belt, Anton Du Beke's enthusiasm for the show remains undimmed, and every new series brings a frisson of excitement for what lies ahead.

'This year is going to be marvellous,' he says. 'When the new cast descend those steps for the first time, we can't wait to see how they get on, how they master the dancing and what they are able to achieve. Throughout the series we all go on that journey with them, and every year brings a whole new host of possibilities.'

The former *Strictly* professional, now a firm favourite on the judges' panel, says the class of 2024 are looking like a 'lovely bunch'.

'I think it's going to be a lot of fun watching how they get on,' he says. 'Both the girls and the boys look interesting, and I'm excited to see all of them strut their stuff.'

Anton is also looking forward to being reunited with his 'gang' of judges – and to another series of sparring with Craig Revel Horwood. He admits, however, that they get on like a house on fire when the cameras stop rolling.

'We're like an old married couple,' he jokes. 'When we're on the *Strictly Come Dancing* Live Tour, we share a car and we share dressing rooms, and he is wonderful. I really enjoy spending time with him. If I need somebody to throw an idea at, I generally turn to Craig. I respect his opinion enormously.'

The new recruits have a lot to live up to after a spectacular Final in 2023, which saw three perfect scores and five 39s awarded by the panel, before Ellie Leach and Vito Coppola won the Glitterball trophy.

'The Grand Final was high class,' says Anton. 'I thought it was great-quality, super dancing. Ellie was so brilliantly consistent. As a judge, you're watching to see all the good bits, but you are also watching to find something that didn't work perfectly because you need something to feed back to them.

'You can say it was marvellous, but sometimes that's not massively helpful. It's better to tell them, "straighten your leg there, or use your heels, because that will take you to the next level." I used to say to my partners, "Don't make it easy for the judges. If they're going to criticise you, make them work for it!"'

As we enter the dance arena for a brand new competition, Anton has sound advice for the celebrity contestants vying for the Glitterball trophy.

'Embrace it, enjoy it as much as you can, because it will be over in a flash, even if you make it all the way to the Final,' he says. 'Wherever you get to in the competition you can be proud that you achieved something that you never thought you'd be able to do. You can't explain to anybody what it's going to be like until they've had a go, and then you enter into the *Strictly* family. I love that expression, because it really is like a family.

'The key to it is to be able to say, "I gave that my all and it was amazing."'

While he's no longer on the professional dancing team, Anton is never far away from his dancing shoes and is hoping he'll be gracing the floor in some of the group routines. 'If I'm asked, I'll be there in a flash,' he laughs.

Anton DU BEKE

Dr Punam KRISHAN

Swapping her scrubs for sequins, Dr Punam Krishan will be hoping to bring a large dose of joy to the ballroom floor – and she is thrilled to be taking part in the show.

'I've been a superfan of the show for years,' she says. 'I've always watched it with my little boy, who is now 11, because it's been our Saturday-night thing. Every year he's said, "You know, Mummy, it would be cool if you did that one day." So it's an amazing feeling to be jumping off the sofa into the telly box and living my best mum life on a Saturday night. This is so out of my comfort zone, but I'm up for the journey and will give it my absolute all.'

Born and raised in Glasgow, Punam went to medical school in the city before becoming an NHS GP. She began her broadcasting career on the BBC Scotland show *Laid Bare*, giving onscreen patients a dressing down about unhealthy lifestyles. Since 2021, she has been a resident GP on BBC's *Morning Live* and BBC Radio Scotland. She regularly reports on health news for TV, radio and national newspapers, and has also written a series of non-fiction children's books.

In preparation for the challenge ahead, Punam, who is paired with Gorka Márquez, has been upping her fitness game.

'I started [the running plan] Couch to 5k, so I'm on week seven and I'm very proud of that,' she says. 'I wasn't a runner before that. I've also been doing a couple of workouts a week at the gym, just to build a bit of stamina. Other than that, I've been prioritising things like getting sleep, eating well and getting ready to start training. I think this will be the fitness journey of our lives.'

The NHS doctor will continue to work and hold surgeries around her training, and says she is still 'figuring out' the timetable to make both work. 'There's going to be a lot of juggling, but I feel it's a perfect balance, because my surgery days are long and can be quite exhausting and frazzling, so I think dancing will be incredible escapism.'

But, with many of her co-presenters on *Morning Live* being *Strictly* alumni, she's had been given plenty of advice herself.

'I'm really lucky because quite a few of my *Morning Live* family members have done the show,' she says. 'Helen Skelton has been incredible. She's like a sister at the minute. I've also got Gethin Jones, Sara Davies and Kimberley Walsh who have all done it, plus Dr Ranj, so I have reached out to all of them and said, "Help!" The one piece of advice I've been hearing consistently has been, "Just enjoy it. It's over before you know it!"'

Not used to being glammed up for her NHS work, Punam reckons a makeover for the show is just what the doctor ordered.

'That's the best bit!' she laughs. 'My life consists of wearing scrubs during the week or leggings and joggers on the weekends, so to go full-on glam has been unreal. I didn't actually recognise myself the day we got *Strictly*-fied for the first time. So, yes, I'm happy to go from scrubs to sparkle. Let's dance!'

Dancing with Dr Punam Krishan, Gorka has prescribed plenty of training and lots of fun. But he says the Scottish GP has just the right dose of enthusiasm.

'Punam is lovely – she's enthusiastic and thrilled to be part of the show,' he says. 'For her, doing *Strictly* is a dream come true. We are both very excited and she has this happy, contagious energy. Everything is new for her and so exciting, so she's passing that feeling on to me. It's like a breath of fresh air.

'I'm so happy to be partnering her and I can't wait to start another journey on *Strictly*.'

The *Morning Live* doctor is not a performer or sports personality, but Gorka sees that as an advantage.

'I think Punam is a rare, truly raw contestant, with no background in entertainment. She's an ordinary, down-to-earth person who works as a GP in the mornings, then takes her scrubs off and goes to her ballroom and Latin heels. But just because she's not a performer doesn't mean that she doesn't have it in her – we just have to bring it out.

We want to go out there and have the best time, and that's the most rewarding thing, because the audience wants to see the celebrities having the best time they can.'

The pair kicked off with a Cha-cha-cha but Gorka thinks Punam will excel in both ballroom and Latin.

'She has been picking up the steps really well and we were dancing the routine to music in the first few days of rehearsal,' he says. 'She has the energy for the Latin and the joyful dances, but I know she can do the ballroom frame because we already did that on the first day.'

Since joining *Strictly* in 2016, Gorka has been a triple finalist with Alexandra Burke, Maisie Smith and Helen Skelton. Born in Bilbao, Spain, he took up dance at 11, representing his country in the World Latin Championships in 2010 and the semi-finals of the 2012 WDSF World Cup. Last year on *Strictly*, he partnered broadcaster Nikita Kanda, leaving in week three.

'Nikita was lovely and fun,' he says. 'We had lots of banter and a lot of jokes together and, although the journey was very short, we had a good time.'

In his ninth series on the show, Gorka is looking forward to celebrating the twentieth anniversary.

'I feel privileged that I can be part of such a big year for *Strictly*, and to be part of a show that is still so loved,' he says. '*Strictly* is for everybody. It's music, dance and pure entertainment. This series' celebrities have the potential to be amazing dancers, but it's also a great variety of different personalities, which is what you want for an entertainment show.'

Hoping to make his fourth Final, Gorka's main goal is to make sure his celebrity partner is left with a smile on her face.

'I want Punam to walk out of *Strictly* and say, "I had the best time of my life."'

Tom DEAN MBE

Fresh from medal glory at the Paris Olympics, Tom Dean is on dry land and going for gold once again. But the Team GB swimmer is feeling like a fish out of water.

'Everything is so new to me,' he says. 'It's exciting, it's different, but dancing couldn't be further from swimming and gravity is something that, all of a sudden, I have got to deal with. Training for sport, learning new techniques, trying to embed them and then performing in a competition is the only parallel I can draw. In terms of dancing, it's a clean slate for me, so who knows? It might be in there somewhere.'

The triple Olympic gold medallist began swimming at eight in his hometown of Maidenhead and studied mechanical engineering at the University of Bath while competing in the pool. Tom made history at the Tokyo 2020 Olympics as the first British man to win a gold medal for the men's 200-metre freestyle in over 100 years. He bagged a second gold as part of the Team GB relay team before becoming England's most-decorated athlete at the 2022 Commonwealth Games, with seven medals. In the 2024 Paris games, he won a third gold medal for Team GB.

Tom follows in the wake of Team GB teammate Adam Peaty, who was a series-19 *Strictly* star, and he has also taken advice from another of the show's legends.

'I chatted to Adam in Paris and I called him a few days ago,' he says. 'He told me," It's so different to swimming," but he also said to enjoy it and make the most of it. I'm good friends with Dan Walker as well and I dropped him a text for a bit of advice. He said, "Just go for it, climb that mountain and enjoy the view."'

The sporting star, who is paired with Nadiya Bychkova, enjoyed getting to know his fellow celebs during the group dance and says he's not yet nervous about the live routines.

'Getting to know everyone has been super-positive and rehearsing the group number was fun,' he says. 'We've also been practising the walkout, onto the stairs, at the beginning of the dance. I think once they announce your name it will actually feel real, and I'm going to have to stand up and do something I've never done before, with no experience whatsoever. That's maybe when I'll think, "Okay, this is serious now," but so far I've loved every minute.

'The first time I saw everybody in costume walking out, saw the lights and the music, I thought it was insane. Obviously, I've watched [the show] on TV, but seeing it in the flesh was amazing.'

While Tom's trophy cabinet is already bulging, he has his eyes on that Glitterball and jokes that it trumps Olympic golds every time.

'If I win, it's going in the centre of the mantlepiece!'

Paired with triple Olympic gold medallist Tom Dean, Nadiya Bychkova plans to make a splash on the dance floor and is hoping to add a Glitterball trophy to his impressive haul of medals.

'I'm so happy and excited to be dancing with him,' she says. 'It's not often you get a chance to teach an Olympic champion, and it's so soon after he won the gold in Paris. He's at the top of his game and it's incredible. It's such a pleasure teaching him and he's a great student because he has an athlete's mindset. He told me that when he's training for the World Championships or Olympics, the coach tells him to do something and he keeps on doing it and repeating it. So the work ethic is there and he just keeps on going.'

While the medal-winning sportsman is at the peak of fitness, the dance floor is a very different environment to the pool, and Nadiya says he's working hard to find his feet.

'In terms of fitness, there's no problem, but on the other hand this is very different to what he is used to doing every day,' she says. 'He is used to being in the pool, but he doesn't do anything on his feet. Last week he went running for the very first time, and now he's very excited to learn to dance. He is really looking forward to it. Because of the mentality he has, he's used to long hours and used to training. Even after a few days of rehearsals, he enjoys it already.'

Ukrainian Nadiya won the Slovenian Ballroom and Latin Championship multiple times and has also been World Champion and European Champion in 'Ten Dance'. She joined *Strictly* in 2017, reaching the quarter-finals with Davood Ghadami. Her previous partners have also included Blue's Lee Ryan, news presenter Dan Walker and Bros star Matt Goss.

Going for gold with her sports-star partner this year, Nadiya is over the moon to be part of the twentieth-birthday celebrations.

'It's amazing,' she says. 'It's incredible, the best show on TV. It brings families together, puts the smile on people's faces.

'It's exciting to be part of the twentieth year and it's a great line-up. They all get on really well and there are a lot of amazing characters. There's a great vibe and energy. What's most important is that they all enjoy the experience, because they only get to do it once.

'I'm looking forward to all of it – teaching, dancing, performing and having the best series ever. Tom's lovely. We're having fun, but at the same time we're putting in the work. It's a wonderful environment, and we get to create a bit of magic on Saturday-night TV.'

Nadiya BYCHKOVA

Clip ART

The live dances are the beating heart of *Strictly*, but the VTs, or videotapes, also play a crucial role in viewers getting to know the celebrities. From the introductory profile films in the launch show to the training-room footage, the pre-recorded segments give fans a glimpse behind the scenes and reveal how their favourite couples are getting on with that week's dance.

The six-strong production team are responsible for co-ordinating and organising all the shoots based on ideas from across the *Strictly* team. In order to get the necessary footage, a team of nine camera operators and nine assistants film upwards of 18 hours of material a week. 'The team goes out in pairs and to all the training rooms, sometimes to multiple different locations in a day,' says Senior Edit Producer Kate Wilkinson. 'Often couples are training in the same space, so one VT shooter can do three training rooms in a day. This year, everyone is more spread out, with people all over the country.

'We spend a lot of time in the rehearsal rooms with the professionals and celebrities and really get to know them. We film within their training day and, during breaks from dancing, we often step in with interview questions and get reactions to things that are going on.

'For some VTs, we take the couples out and about. For example, if it's Movie Week, they might go to the cinema or come up with film-related location ideas. But the stories that come through training are the most important part and will make up about 80 per cent of what we shoot. We follow how the dances are going and [talk about] that in the interview. The VT is a brilliant snapshot of those fun moments.'

For the videos shot outside of the rehearsal spaces, the ideas can come from the most unexpected places, from the runners to the shooting producer directors. 'There's a forward-planning team, VT Series Producer Ciara Murray, the exec producers and myself, and we all muck in,' says Kate. 'We also have a story producer who feeds through information, which might come from conversations in the corridor with a celebrity. For example, this year we found out that Wynne Evans used to be a sumo wrestler, so we take that and start creating it into an idea, then we pitch to Executive Producer Sarah James once a week and start filming the following week.'

The weeks running up to the launch show are among the busiest for the team, with 15 celebrity profiles, 15 pairings and the previous winner's VT. This year the profiles were filmed in 15 different locations, each one special to the celebrity, while the couples were paired, three or four at a time, at stunning dance locations around the country.

'We sent people out to shoot the profiles, and the following week we shot all the pairing VTs,' says Kate. 'They are then cut over the next week, ready to feed into the launch recording so the studio audience can watch them and get a sense of everyone who's in the competition this year.

The Blackpool Special means shipping everything 250 miles north and a very special assignment. 'We have a crew there from Monday and we film the transformation of the Tower Ballroom into the *Strictly* ballroom,' says Kate. 'It's an amazing week because you can feel, both on- and off-screen, how much it means to the celebrities to get to that point. That excitement and the amazing energy really translate when we're filming. Also, we can go on the Big Dipper and take couples to places that might be nostalgic for them, so it's always a fun one. But we often have to get the rides reopened because the attractions are shut down for the winter, or we need to find a donkey in November, which requires a bit of planning!

'My favourite week is Movie Week' though, because we can really take inspiration from the films. One year, we opened the show with a *Mission Impossible*-style VT, which was great, and we see such amazing creativity from everyone. Halloween is also really great fun.'

A Week in the Life of the VT Team

MONDAY

We go in and film the celebrities and the professionals talking about how the weekend went, first of all. Then we start filming as they begin their new routine and establish what they're going to be doing that week, and we get their thoughts and feelings on that.

TUESDAY

We continue following the training and pick up on any steps they might be finding tricky. The edit starts as well, with editors cutting all the things we shot on Monday.

WEDNESDAY

We tend to shoot the out-and-about VTs on a Wednesday. As there are two days of footage at this point the VT editors are able to start seeing how the story for the week will come together and, if needed, give us some direction on what else should be shot.

THURSDAY

For the camera team, Thursday's a pick-up day. We can get any shots that have been suggested and we continue to build on the story. It's when the VTs are really taking shape in the edit.

FRIDAY

All the VTs are completed and sent to the executives to be signed off late on a Friday night.

SATURDAY

We colour-correct all the videos on a Saturday, then they go straight out. It's quite a quick turnaround, but we work really closely with the editors and the camera team to make sure that it's a cohesive unit and we have exactly what we need in time for the live show on Saturday night.

After wowing the judges with her incredible routines with Vito Coppola, series-20 finalist Fleur East swapped hats for her debut as *It Takes Two* presenter last year. And she had a whale of a time working with co-host Janette Manrara.

'It was so much fun and I felt instantly at home,' she says. 'Everybody made me feel welcome and, because I joined *It Takes Two* just after dancing in *Strictly*, I knew all the professionals, I knew the whole team, so it felt really comfortable.

'Janette is as silly as me, so when it came to filming the trailers and skits, like the *Mission Impossible* and *The Shining* scenes, it was so much fun. We were like big kids.'

The chart-topping singer has fallen naturally into her new role and says she has become the *It Takes Two* number cruncher.

'I love being on *It Takes Two* because I get to see all the stats, and that's really interesting,' she says. 'We see who danced the highest-scoring Samba, who's broken records, who's getting the most 10s and so on, which I love. But most of all, I like sitting down with the couples and chatting.'

Having been in their shoes, Fleur can't wait to see the new cast of celebrities take their first steps and try out the different dance styles. 'I think the line-up is amazing this year,' she says. 'There's a nice mixture of characters and I think we're going to have some big performances. I'm excited to see everyone hit the ballroom floor because there are always surprises. Every year there are people that you underestimate until you see them move.

'There are plenty of names to watch out for, I don't think you should underestimate anybody on the list. There are always a lot of surprises.

Having reached the Final with Vito, Fleur was over the moon to see him land the title of *Strictly* champion with Ellie Leach in his second year on the show.

'Vito's like a little brother to me now. He's family. We talk nearly every day, so when I watched him win, I was so emotional. I cried my eyes out. I was so pleased for him and it was well deserved. Vito and Ellie had a great partnership and you could see her growth through the series.'

'It's a huge privilege to be so close to the action, because I feel like my *Strictly* experience continues and never ends. I feel very lucky to be part of it.'

Paul MERSON

Former Arsenal ace Paul Merson is looking to score some big points from the judges – but as a TV pundit who dishes out the odd criticism in the football realm, he'll be able to take their comments on his own moves.

'In my job, I'm the one giving the feedback. Now I'm going to get it!' he laughs. 'But if the criticism is fair, I respect that. I'll take it on the chin.'

Making his debut for Arsenal FC at 17, Paul went on to win the PFA Young Player of the Year. He stayed with the club for over a decade, playing 424 times, scoring 99 goals and helping them win domestic trophies as well as the European Cup Winners' Cup. He also played 21 times for England and has had stints at Middlesbrough, Aston Villa and Portsmouth, before becoming player-manager at Walsall FC. Now a sports pundit, Paul has written numerous bestselling books that cover his football career and personal life, including *How Not to Be a Professional Footballer*.

The Londoner is a close friend of ex-footballer Tony Adams, who danced in series 20 and offered him some advice on his *Strictly* journey.

'Tony told me I would be nervous before the dances, but I'm going to tackle this challenge head on and I'm hoping my two left feet can learn some moves.

'As a footballer, I was decent at that, but this is so far out of my comfort zone. I've started a couple of dances so far and I've definitely still got some work to do!'

For the costumes Paul adds, 'I might wear a sparkly vest or something tight, but unlike Tony, I'm not planning to take off my shirt!'

Paired with Karen Hauer, Paul is hoping his skills on the pitch will translate onto the dance floor.

'Hopefully, I'll be okay on my feet – I've been on them all my life,' he says. 'You need to have some coordination on a football pitch, and that's crucial on the dance floor too. A good coach and quality teaching are the most important things. One lesson I learned from football is to always be around good players.'

As someone who has spent most of his Saturday nights watching the beautiful game, London-born Paul admits he has been caught off-guard by the incredible reaction to his participation in *Strictly*.

'I hadn't thought about the impact of the show because I try to live my life a day at a time and don't worry about stuff until it happens,' he says. 'But it's amazing how many people come up and talk to you about it. I'm just starting to realise how huge the show is. It is mind-blowing.'

Dancing with former footballer Paul Merson, Karen Hauer is hoping to hit the back of the net with their high-energy routines and is having a ball in rehearsals.

'Paul is fun to work with, and because of his athletic background, he's really light on his feet,' she says. 'He pays attention because he's used to being coached, and he has also coached, so he understands how important it is to listen. He's a great student so far. Obviously dancing is new to him, so it's about getting that musicality and the confidence.

'He also has a really good sense of humour. We have a lot of banter and fun, and still get our heads down and work. He always comes in happy and positive, so I'm really enjoying his energy.'

Karen is hoping Paul's skills on the pitch will help him tackle the dance-floor moves.

'Paul was so used to being on his feet, being light and changing direction quickly, so that helps in using his core and spatial awareness, but also he's really good at focusing on what he has to do,' she says. 'He's used to being on TV and playing in front of big crowds, so that has never fazed him. Obviously, he's out of his comfort zone right now, but if I can relate it as much as I can to football, he actually feels pretty comfortable.'

The pair kicked off with an American Smooth, meaning the sports pundit had to learn some tricky lifts in week one. But Karen says he takes it all in his stride.

'I threw everything into our first dance because we have more time to train before the first live show, so it's easier to digest,' she says. 'There were some difficult lifts and technique, but he handled it well.

'Paul is up for the judges' comments as well. He understands that the judges know what they're looking at and all he can do is try his best. I like his mindset.'

Born in Valencia, Venezuela, Karen began dancing at the age of eight, later moving to New York to study African dance, contemporary and ballet before specialising in ballroom and Latin at 19. Now the longest-serving professional in *Strictly*, having joined in 2012, she has reached the Final twice, with Mark Wright and Jamie Laing. Last year, she partnered comedian Eddie Kadi.

'Eddie was a ball of fun, very happy and upbeat', she says. 'Even when we were just sitting down we were laughing, and he always had something funny to say, hence why we're still friends today.'

Entering her thirteenth year on *Strictly*, Karen says her time on the show has flown, but every series brings fresh excitement.

'I'm always very grateful and I don't take for granted the fact that I've been brought back for 13 series,' she says. 'I'm so happy that I get to do my job and to help my partners find their confidence. I just love the work, I love the job, I love getting in there and teaching, I love the progress the celebrities make, and I love being in the studio.

'*Strictly* also has the most amazing fans. A lot of them have grown up with us and, from generation to generation, they keep watching the show. So we have a responsibility to keep making the memories and put on the best show we can.

'The dynamic of the cast is different every year and the class of 2024 are heart-warming, funny and ready to go for it. I think it's going to be a great year. I feel very privileged to be here.

Karen HAUER

Double TAKE

A Day in the Life of the *It Takes Two* Team

When it comes to *Strictly Come Dancing*, the fun doesn't end when the lights go down at the weekend. Throughout the week, the *It Takes Two* team are on hand to keep the ballroom buzz going, with live interviews, features and fascinating *Strictly* stats. Here, presenters Janette Manrara and Fleur East talk us through a day on the *ITT* set.

JANETTE

2 p.m.: I arrive at the studio and the first thing I do is have a coffee, then I have a script meeting with my producer. We sit down and talk through the running order, the questions that we're going to be asking the couples, any kind of videos (VTs) we're going to be playing. Between the two of us, we lock down exactly what the show is going to be for the day.

2.45 p.m.: After that's done, I head down to the studio, still dressed in my own clothes – normally something comfortable like jeans and a big jumper. We do a very slow run-through of the entire show so the camera crew can make sure they're in the right positions and getting the right shots. I also have to work out my positions for each section, so I'll be asking questions like, 'Am I coming in from this side today?' It also gives me a chance to rehearse the questions I'll be asking the couples coming in as guests. What I really love about the rehearsal is that our producers and researchers pretend they are the couples. So, for example, if the guests were Annabel Croft and Johannes Radebe, we'll have one crew member acting as Johannes and one acting as Annabel, and they really go for it! They talk about their life, training and the dances at the weekend and I love how invested they are in delivering their role.

5 p.m.: I go back up to my dressing room and grab a bite to eat, then I'm in hair and make-up. So we have a good natter while the make up artist works her magic, but I'll also run through the show again on my own, while I'm in the chair.

At this point, the producers are briefing the couples and letting them know if they want them to do something fun on the set.

6.15 p.m.: Once I've done my final hair and make-up check and talked to the producer about any changes that may have come up after speaking to the couples, the sound guys come up to my room, mic me up and give me an earpiece.

I'm a social media queen, so I always try to do a post just before I go live, to get everybody excited to tune in and watch. Sometimes it's in my make-up chair, sometimes in wardrobe or on set, but we're tight on time so I try to do it in one shot and keep it fun. I get on to set 10 minutes before we go live, and we do a quick rehearsal of the opening link.

6.30 p.m.: I give a big, 'Cheers to everyone. Have a great show,' and we are live. With live telly, as you can imagine, anything can change, almost on the spot. Sometimes, while a VT is playing, I'll be getting notes from my producer saying, 'We're going to change this item,' so you have to be ready. I love live television for that reason, because it keeps it exciting!

Because I have an autocue, I don't have to remember the script – and I can let you into a little secret. When I'm chatting to the guests I don't use cue cards, because I am too invested and I like using my hands a lot, so I have a sneaky little screen on the side of the sofa. It's a very small monitor, a mini autocue, but only I can see it. It means I never have to take my eyes away from the couples for long if I want to have a quick prompt for the next question.

My favourite part of the show is chatting with the couples. You want to get their take on their performance and find out how they feel. It's also great to get an exclusive sneak peek into what we're about to watch the following Saturday night. But I also love the footage that shows the behind-the-scenes stuff about how the professional dances come together, and taking viewers into the gallery where the director sits to see all the camera shots at once. That's the kind of insider insight that audiences can only get on *It Takes Two*, and it gives viewers an appreciation for how much hard work goes into creating the show.

FLEUR

2 p.m.: After arriving at the *It Takes Two* studio, the producer and I have a little briefing in the dressing room, and we go through the entire script together, take things out and make any amendments. I make a lot of notes while watching the Saturday show, jotting down things that I want to ask the couples the following week, which helps. When we're done we go down [to the studio] and do two run-throughs of the whole show from start to finish, making notes where necessary.

5 p.m.: After the second run-through, I go back up to my dressing room to get my hair and make-up done for the evening. Once I get glammed up it feels real because I'm in uniform, ready to go. I also like to go and chat to the guests when they arrive and see how they're feeling before we go on.

6.30 p.m.: Showtime. There's a lot of prep that goes into the show on the day even before we get there, but the real adrenaline rush starts when the camera starts rolling. I don't use cue cards because I like to look at people when I'm talking to them so I have the questions in my head before I get out there and I can just fire them out. Also, if the celeb says something really interesting, I will riff off that, because they often tell you things that are unexpected, so you've got to be ready to roll with it.

people are geared up for the show the next day, and I get to chat with everyone.

Having danced in the competition myself, I know exactly what the celebs are going through – which muscles are aching, for example, in a Jive week – so it's great to chat with them and give them a bit of encouragement. I had an absolute blast on the show and now my *Strictly* experience continues through *It Takes Two*, and I feel so lucky to be part of it.

7 p.m.: Show's over and what happens next depends on the day of the week. If it's a Monday, when a couple have been eliminated, the mood may be a little sad. If it's a Friday, there's a huge buzz in the studio. It's a real party atmosphere because

Sam QUEK MBE

She spent years on the hockey pitch, competing at international level, but Olympic gold medallist Sam Quek is now ready to tackle a new challenge.

'The thought of dancing on the ballroom floor in front of a live audience is quite daunting, but I'm up for it,' she says. 'This is the perfect time for me. My kids love it and enjoy it – and also, I can't wait for the glow-up!'

The sports star and mum to three-year-old Molly and two-year-old Isaac admits the sparkles and sequins of the *Strictly Come Dancing* wardrobe are a far cry from her usual tracksuits and trainers – but she's embracing the change.

'It's overwhelming at first,' she says. 'When I did my first photoshoot, I was uncomfortable because it's so much hair and make-up, you've got sequins, a little bit of leg on show. I'm just not used to that. But when you're in front of the camera with the music, and the lights go on, it's all part of the *Strictly* persona.

Born in Liverpool, Sam won 125 international caps for the England and Great Britain women's hockey teams, and was part of the team that landed a gold medal at the 2016 Rio Olympics. A year later, she was awarded an MBE for Services to Hockey. She went on to a career in broadcasting, presenting BBC's *Morning Live* and various sports shows covering football, American football, rugby and cricket. She co-anchored the BBC's Tokyo Olympic Games coverage in 2021, alongside her *Strictly* 'hero' Dan Walker, and the same year she became a team captain on *A Question of Sport*.

Her sporting background will help in training, but Sam says professional partner Nikita Kuzmin 'will have to have loads of patience, like a good lunch and be up for a laugh – but also be able to say, "Sam, concentrate now," because I can get carried away.'

Sam found remembering the steps in the first group dance was her first challenge of the competition.

'It's been a real whirlwind,' she says. 'It was a slow burn after finding out we were going to be on the show, but as soon as we were all together, this big group of celebrities and professionals, it was really exciting.

'Learning the first group dance was fun but hard. Twice, in rehearsals, I experienced a complete mind blank, where I got to a part in the dance and there's nothing there. Nikita reassured me it's a normal process and that we have a whole week for the individual dances, instead of the two days we had for the group dance. So far, I'm enjoying every single minute.'

Sam's friends and family are 'buzzing' about her stint on the *Strictly* dance floor, and some of them have even got quite emotional. 'One of my best friends cried,' she says. Now, after taking her first steps in the rehearsal room, she is feeling the buzz herself.

'I'm chuffed to be a part of this legendary show,' she says. 'It feels absolutely surreal, but I'm ready for every bit of the adventure.'

Series 21 finalist Nikita Kuzmin is paired with Olympic gold medallist Sam Quek and says her background in sport is making rehearsal time a dream.

'Sam's doing really well and training hard,' he says. 'I'm very impressed by her work ethic and commitment. She absorbs the information so quickly, which I'm assuming is because of her sports background. She's an Olympic champion, so she must have had that training ethic instilled in her.

'She has been absolutely 100 per cent committed since day one. Even at times when I stop teaching her, she's still going on her own, repeating steps, repeating her frame. She's constantly training in the background.'

While the hockey star-turned-presenter is super-fit, Nikita says training can still be challenging. 'What helps is having coordination, which is obviously a massive factor in dancing, but in terms of fitness, dancing requires a very different kind of fitness,' he says.

Nikita was just four when he took up dancing in his native Ukraine and later in Italy, where his family moved when he was nine. He is a six-time Italian National Champion and, at 18, he moved to Germany to dance as a professional. He joined *Strictly* in series 19, and last year he was a runner-up in the Grand Final with actor Layton Williams.

'The talent that guy has is incredible,' he says. 'Anything you ask, any dance style, any acrobatic turn, leg movement, character, personality – Layton has it all. I was really lucky to be paired with him.

We spent almost the whole year together, because we did *Strictly*, then the *Strictly Come Dancing* Live Tour. Layton is one of my best friends. Everybody knows him as this extraordinary dancer, but he's also an extraordinary person.'

The pair scored 39 for their Argentine Tango and bagged a perfect score for their Paso Doble and Charleston before reaching the Grand Final.

'My favourite dance we performed is probably our Paso Doble because it was our first 40. It's one of those moments you remember forever.'

As he enters his fourth year, Nikita pays tribute to the *Strictly* fans who have been loyal to the show for two decades.

'I feel lucky to be asked back every year to do the job of my dreams,' he says. 'We are truly in a lucky position, and for the twentieth anniversary I feel even more joy, pride and gratitude.

'I love meeting fans. It's wonderful so see how happy the special moments make people, and when somebody says what that means to them personally. Just to see us two boys dancing meant a lot to so many people. It's amazing to meet people whose hearts you have touched. That's why it's the best job in the world!'

Nikita KUZMIN

With two decades of judging on the show under his belt, Craig Revel Horwood knows a thing or two about what makes a winner on *Strictly Come Dancing*.

'The most important thing to remember is to practise and make it muscle memory,' he says. 'You have to know those routines inside out so you're able to perform them without thinking of the steps, entertain people and enjoy the dance. That way your personality will shine through, and that is more important than getting the steps, especially in the early stages.

'Also, take on board all the judges' comments and always listen to your professional, because they've been dancing all their life, some from the age of three, so they are full of good advice. But mostly, practise, practise, practise.'

The distinguished judge reckons the latest cast of celebrities are a 'great bunch' and says the launch show was a barrel of laughs. But he also cast a knowing eye over the new recruits.

'The launch show was a great success and it was wonderful seeing the celebrities dance for the first time,' Craig continues. 'This year we've got Olympians, sportsmen, singers, comedians. Each contestant has their own skills and experience that they can lean on and of course their own set of challenges too. I can't wait to how each of them perform each week. I really hope there's some excellent dancing too, otherwise I'll naturally have something to say about that!'

At the launch show it was also revealed that Craig has pulled out his 1 paddle 10 times through the last two decades. But he admits his 10 paddle is also getting more of a show these days.

'Jill Halfpenny set the bar with her Jive in series two,' he says. 'That was the first time I'd ever got the 10 paddle out and it was in the Final, so there were no 10s in series one. I think from series three, celebs came in knowing what to expect and the bar was raised. Since then the standard has got steadily better. Last year, for example, Layton was just incredible, and I awarded five 10s.'

Craig says the series-21 Grand Final, won by Ellie Leach, was an unforgettable show and proves that the public rightly have the last word.

'Ellie was fantastic – she won the hearts and minds of the nation,' he says. 'I think when Ellie came out and did her Paso Doble she won everybody over, and from that moment on, they were rooting for her.'

This year, Craig is thrilled to see Amy Dowden and Aljaž Škorjanec back on the *Strictly* dance floor. 'It's wonderful that Amy is better and able to dance again, and I think she's inspiring so many people who are going through cancer treatment,' he says. 'She's back, she's vibrant, and she's so happy to be on that dance floor.

'Aljaž is as great at talking as he is at dancing. He's a big personality, so it's wonderful to have one of our family favourites back in the fold again, too.'

Craig REVEL HORWOOD

Setting the SCENE

Whether it's a Tango in a wood-panelled Argentinian bar or a cheeky funfair-themed Charleston with a 15-foot pink teddy-bear rack, the staging of *Strictly Come Dancing* routines sets the tone and helps tell the story of each dance.

As well as being stunning to look at, these incredible transformations, created by Performance Designer Catherine Land and her amazing team, have to be set in under two minutes on the live show, so design is key. And with up to 15 couples' dances and two professional group dances per week, that's no mean feat.

'I've worked on the show for 11 years and the staging has become much bigger and more ambitious,' says Catherine. 'We still have the classic lamppost and bench for some numbers but it's interspersed with huge, tech-heavy builds with lots of LED and a lot more staging, rather than just props. So instead of having an umbrella, a couple might have a full exotic bar set-up or be on an amazing neon structure that rotates. If the story unfolds in a bistro, where we used to have one table and chair, I might now build the full bistro backing with several window flats and lots of tables and chairs instead of just the one.'

For Catherine, work starts in mid-July when the concepts for the group dances begin to come together and she can begin to put pen to paper.

'The professional numbers often have the biggest builds because there are so many dancers,' says Catherine. 'The biggest we have ever done was the *Encanto* house, in series 20, which went right to the top of the screens in the studio. It had six windows, including one right at the top where dancers could pop out. It was very complicated behind it because we had to use a lot of rigging to make it safe. We had to build the entire thing in the studio.'

Concepts for the couples' dances, however, are not finalised until the Saturday before each live show, and Catherine can still be making tweaks – and even ordering whole new builds – right up to the wire.

'Just before the Saturday show goes live, we have a sit-down and nail all the ideas for the following week,' she explains. 'None of us can really finalise plans for the next week until then. 'I work with the dance team and they'll tell me the concept – for example, an amusement arcade or a bar – and give me some references relevant to the dance and song, like a Salsa would be bright and colourful, for instance. Then I'll go away and design the staging. I always think about including LED or lighting into the builds, so if it affects our Lighting Designer, Dave Bishop, I'll give him a call to say, "I have six practical lights on this," or, "I have festoon [lights] on this," just to warn him. I also liaise with the LED crew, who come under my banner.

'Once I have a design I send it over to the senior producers and then to the construction. All this happens in the space of a day.'

Catherine has two carpenters and a painter on her team to help with the builds, but also uses outside construction companies when there is a heavy workload, as well as bringing in extra painters.

'I have a brilliant set dresser called Caroline Berry-Reid, who puts the finishing touches to the set,' says Catherine. 'So if I've built a bakery, she'll fill it with all the breads needed, or if it's a florist, she'll acquire lots of flowers to make it all look pretty.'

With scenery having to be swapped over between dances, Catherine works with Scenic Supervisor Mark Osborne on the practicalities of getting the builds on and off the dance floor.

'I'll tell Mark what's coming up in the week, and he'll say, "Can we have that bar on wheels?" or "Can this be made in three sections?" We also have to take storage into account, because we don't have a lot of space backstage. It's like a Tetris game, working out what can go in there. Mark has a crew of between six and eight, who do a brilliant job of organising it, making sure everything is stacked in the right order to get access when each item is needed.'

The choreography of each dance plays a huge part in the design, of course, and Catherine consults with the professional dancers to make sure each item works – which can lead to some last-minute changes. 'On one occasion we made an *Aladdin* sofa, but the dancers had been using a different sofa [in rehearsal] that was not the same size or shape,' she says. 'When they saw it they said, "We have to kneel on the arm," but our sofa had a curved arm so they couldn't. We often have to remake items to suit the dancers' specific requirements. It could be that they need a block to get up onto a platform, a step is a bit too high, or they need a hidden handle to help them.'

With technical rehearsals taking place on Friday, Catherine has to think on her feet to come up with clever solutions. 'We start getting basic units at the beginning of the week, but then we do the rest in the studio, and we're only there from Thursday onwards,' she says. 'We rebuild sets from scratch as late as the Friday. One time, we hired a bus shelter, but it was just too big for our dance floor, so on Friday I said, "I'm calling it: we're building it from scratch." We were all flying around, with the chippies building the shelter, the LED crew adding the lights and all of us adding the decoration.'

With 15 couples all hoping to make a splash, week one often has many builds for Catherine's team.

'If it's not a themed week, I normally have a rule that up to two-thirds of the dances can have props, but in week one, there might be more as the cast is established,' she explains. 'So if the celebrity is a tennis player, there could be a tennis-themed set and so on. But sometimes a simple, elegant dance is better without too much staging.'

'Some routines are very choreo-heavy on the build, with lots of dancers,' says Catherine. 'For example, if there are platforms, you have to make sure everyone can get up to them via hidden back treads, or if someone has to jump down, you have to make sure it is weight-bearing. But the trickiest is when it involves flat-wall scenery that moves during the routine. Bobby Brazier and Dianne Buswell had movable walls [in 2023] for their showdance to *La La Land*, where they start off in front of a brick wall, which parts and they dance onto the rest of the floor.

'The flats are on wheels and have handles behind and there are eight crew members hiding behind them. As soon as they hit the right beat, they have to move them out of the way, so everyone has to hit the right mark. But it's fun when they are involved. We may have one of the guys hide in a bar all routine and pass a glass up on cue, or they are controlling trap doors or popping out of toaster lifts. They're fun to do.

'Another challenge is when we have people flying in with giant wings or on a roller-coaster car – which we once built – because you have to get them specially made for the riggers. One of my favourites was when Frankie Bridge flew up at the end of her *Wicked* Tango with a broomstick [in 2014], and huge swags of green fabric had been draped over the stairs but seemed to come out of nowhere!'

Nick KNOWLES

As the presenter of *DIY SOS*, Nick Knowles has been changing lives for 25 years by helping to rebuild homes. After meeting Anton Du Beke and some of the professional dancers for an *SOS* special last year, he's ready to cement his place on the *Strictly* leaderboard.

'I really enjoyed spending time with the dancers and with Anton,' he says. 'They were all encouraging me to go for it, and I was toying with the idea. Plus, I just love challenges. Each time I've got to a certain point in my career, I want to try something new. I did 10 years in news and then went into light entertainment, did 12 years of Saturday-night TV, then made a film. So I jumped at the chance to do something completely different again because that's how you stay alive, engaged and excited about the world.'

Born in Middlesex, Nick began his TV career as a production runner before becoming a local news reporter and presenter. As well as fronting the BBC's BAFTA-winning *DIY SOS* since 1999, he has presented numerous prime-time shows, including *Who Dares Wins*, *Last Choir Standing* and *Perfection*. Passionate about travelling, he has recently fronted a variety of travel programmes.

Despite his many talents, Nick reckons partner Luba Mushtuk will have her work cut out. 'I've spent my life playing rugby and running into people, so I'm not sure if I can be light on my feet, but I hope to find out over the next few weeks. I hope that people will stick by me as I learn.'

Nick recently tried out a few Argentine Tango steps on a trip to Patagonia and found he loved it, so he's looking forward to learning more.

'I'm quite a fan of the ballet and musicals, and there's that fantastic sequence in *Moulin Rouge*, the "Roxanne" sequence, where they're pretty much doing a variation of the Argentine Tango. I've always thought that was an amazing piece of theatre. To be able to produce something like that would be brilliant.

'Also, the Waltz is a beautiful thing and my mother, who passed away 30 years ago, absolutely loved the Waltz and dancing in general.'

With his eye on the main prize, Nick is taking his inspiration from past winner Bill Bailey. 'Bill is probably my favourite past contestant because I didn't expect he could dance,' he says. 'But I love the fact he went in there saying, "I'm going to go for it." And then he went and won it.'

Having shed the builders' boots and hard hat for the sparkly jackets and Cuban heels, Nick is ready to go the whole hog – even if it means a ribbing from the *DIY SOS* crew. 'There's no point coming into *Strictly* and not being ready and willing to go for the *Strictly* makeover,' he says. 'But me turning up on site with a tan, I am going to get some proper stick for that!'

Dad-of-four Nick is determined to throw himself into learning a new skill and to make his family and friends proud. 'I've got kids watching so I want to try and do well enough that I don't embarrass them,' he says. 'But I'm so, so excited to be doing *Strictly* this year. Dancing live on TV will be a whole new adventure, but I've never been afraid of a challenge. There's life in the old dog yet.'

Professional Luba Mushtuk showcased her home-improvement skills on the *DIY SOS Strictly Special* last year, which saw Anton and a team from the show helping to renovate an inclusive arts centre in the Northeast. Now she is turning the tables on presenter Nick Knowles and putting him through his paces in the training room – after sharing a few steps with him on the build.

'I was very happy to be partnered with Nick because I met him on *DIY SOS*,' she says. 'He made me work very hard, but I love doing DIY. I actually had a little dance with Nick as well. I thought at that time that he could be really good.'

The TV presenter has made a good first impression on his new tutor, throwing himself into the training from day one.

'We had an amazing first day,' she says. 'And he's carried on with that enthusiasm. In the early days, there's a lot of information for the celebrities.'

With their first live couple's dance falling on Nick's birthday, Luba made sure their Jive was a fitting celebration.

'The Jive is pretty full-on but I wanted him to have fun with it,' she says. 'I wanted it to be a birthday present of a dance, so he could go out there and have the best time. Nick really wants to do well and he really wants to dance.'

While Nick is happy to give Latin his all, Luba thinks ballroom might be where he finds his natural fit.

'I think when Nick is in hold, he will be very elegant in posture,' she says. 'But with each dance, I take it one day at a time, and when we get to that bridge, we'll cross it.'

Born in St Petersburg, Luba moved to Italy at 12 to study dance and is four-time winner of the Italian Dance Championship and Italian Open Latin Show Dance Champion. She joined the *Strictly Come Dancing* professional team in series 16 and partnered James Cracknell and Jason Bell before dancing with actor Adam Thomas in series 21.

As always, Luba is hoping to make the Final with her celebrity partner, but she says: 'You can never tell who has the potential to go all the way, people always surprise me, and I do believe that Nick is one of those who will surprise all of us,' she says. 'Obviously, I hope we will get to the Final, but I will take it week by week, dance by dance. What's important for me is that he finds the passion and the bravery to dance, and hopefully he will keep dancing after this programme.'

As she enters her seventh series as a professional on the show, Luba is delighted to be part of the twentieth-anniversary celebrations.

'It's fantastic. It's a celebration of this show, which brings joy to so many people. I am just so lucky and grateful to be part of the most joyous programme on the TV.'

Luba MUSHTUK

As an eight-year-old boy, Kai Widdrington remembers watching the first series of *Strictly Come Dancing* – and being inspired to become a professional dancer.

'I remember watching the show for the first time with my grandma and mum,' he says. 'It was the family show on Saturday night that we all watched together. I watched all the original cast, thinking, "That's the way I'm supposed to do the Cha-cha-cha or the Samba." *Strictly* has always been there, so to be here and part of the show 20 years on feels incredible. I feel privileged.'

Southampton-born Kai was World Junior Latin American Champion at the age of 14. He was also a professional on Ireland's *Dancing with the Stars*, reaching the Final twice, before joining the UK show in 2021, dancing with AJ Odudu. Last year, he partnered TV legend Angela Rippon – who went viral in week one with her incredible leg extension in their opening Cha-cha-cha.

'Angela was an absolute dream. I couldn't have asked for anyone better,' he says. 'Angela changed my life in so many ways, and I've got a friend for life. She is the most amazing person.

'My dad told me to watch the Morecambe and Wise clip where Angela comes out from behind a news desk and dances, so I asked Angela if she was still that flexible and she said, "Why don't I find out?" So we did. It ended up being this iconic moment and was in every national newspaper!'

However, Kai's favourite dance with Angela was the Argentine Tango.

'We loved the Argentine Tango, because she danced so beautifully and her technique was incredible,' he says. 'Craig gave us a nine and she's 79! He doesn't just give those out easily. But we had a ball. Every week was fun. It was such an honour to work with her. She's a true legend.

'Seeing Angela on the *Strictly Come Dancing* Live Tour was fantastic too. I told her at the start to cherish every moment, and it was really great fun.'

From his first day on the show, Kai says *Strictly Come Dancing* changed his life, with fans wanting selfies and keen to talk to him about his partners.

'The format's devised fantastically well and people get behind the professionals as well as the celebrities, but they also love Tess, Claudia, the judges, Dave Arch and the live band,' he says. 'I think it's so special. Winning the National Television Award [for Best Talent Show] this year proved how much people enjoy this glittery, bubbly show.'

Although not dancing with a celebrity partner this year, Kai thinks we're in for a bumper series. 'It's a fantastic line-up. There are some great people in the cast and they are definitely going to be entertaining, but there is also lots of potential. We might be in for a few surprises.

'I'm going to be there cheering on my colleagues and I'm looking forward to the group dances and dancing to some amazing musical artists, as well as doing the Christmas special. It's going to be a great series.'

Kai WIDDRINGTON

Word SEARCH

1. Judge who hails from South Africa *(5, 6)*

2. Latin dance that gets the party started *(5)*

3. *EastEnders* star and series-21 finalist *(5, 7)*

4. Dance that can be Argentinian or ballroom *(5)*

5. Professional partner of number 3 *(6, 7)*

6. Studio where the show is filmed *(7)*

7. Helen, who danced into the Final of series 20 with an incredible *Cabaret* routine *(7)*

8. Soap actress who took Anton all the way to the Final *(4, 6)*

9. Angela, who partnered Carlos Gu in series 21 *(7)*

10. *Strictly*'s longest-serving professional dancer *(5, 5)*

11. Everyone wants to be top of this at the end of the Saturday show *(11)*

12. *It Takes Two* star Janette *(7)*

13. Presenter and series-17 finalist Mr Zeroual *(5)*

14. Ms McDermott, series-21 contestant *(4)*

15. Series-20 star Mr Mellor *(4)*

16. Mr Márquez, dancer who partnered number 7 *(5)*

X	L	E	A	D	E	R	B	O	A	R	D	D	S	C
S	A	M	B	A	B	N	M	V	I	C	V	L	A	G
R	D	O	O	M	O	Y	R	O	T	K	C	B	O	L
A	W	Q	U	T	R	P	H	O	I	N	E	G	J	L
W	O	P	L	K	S	C	A	N	L	O	N	U	P	E
D	A	E	F	E	C	I	X	M	P	A	L	L	I	W
N	K	A	R	I	M	K	M	J	T	L	K	Q	Y	S
S	R	M	A	R	Q	U	M	A	N	R	A	R	A	U
O	O	X	R	E	I	Z	A	R	B	Y	B	B	O	B
I	G	W	I	L	F	A	B	R	K	U	G	T	V	E
N	O	C	K	S	T	R	A	U	S	Q	S	B	O	N
C	N	N	O	T	R	A	B	A	M	M	E	E	K	N
P	I	X	V	R	O	G	K	F	U	I	K	D	U	A
T	K	T	F	E	X	J	U	I	C	H	M	U	O	I
R	K	A	R	E	N	H	A	U	E	R	P	Q	P	D
G	B	W	A	O	G	H	B	I	L	D	P	A	I	L

In his first year on *Strictly Come Dancing*, Carlos Gu made the Final with Molly Rainford, and last year he danced his way to week 10 with TV presenter Angela Scanlon.

'I had the best time meeting Angela, and I felt so lucky,' he says. 'We are still close friends now.'

The couple pulled off some unforgettable routines, including an impressive week-three Charleston, which earned 35 points, and an iconic Argentine Tango in Blackpool, which scored them three 10s.

'Angela is funny, she's bold and so smart,' says Carlos. 'She picked up some dances really quickly and was amazing.

'The Charleston felt like a breakthrough moment and she it did perfectly. It was a "wow" moment because it was only week three and she was already showing her talent, her acting skills, and it was amazing.

'My favourite dance was our Argentine Tango in Blackpool. We were the only couple who didn't have extra dancers, only the two of us.'

The couple took both dances on the *Strictly Come Dancing* Live Tour, and got an incredible response from the fans in every venue.

'The *Strictly Come Dancing* Live Tour was fun and we got a chance to do our favourite dances. The reaction to our Argentine Tango from the audience was incredible.'

Carlos, from Taiyuan, China, started dancing at 11 and studied dance at Tianjin University of Sport and the Beijing Dance Academy. At 14, he came third in the German Open Championship and he went on to become Chinese National Latin Champion and Asian Champion. He joined *Strictly* in 2022 and says dancing on the show is still a dream come true.

'*Strictly* is so special. It's just brilliant to be part of it, and I'm buzzing to be back. I'm so lucky.'

While the new batch of celebrities may be feeling first-night nerves, Carlos has some sound advice.

'Everybody feels a little bit self-conscious at the start, but I would say go out there and dance like nobody's watching,' he says. 'Have fun, and just embrace it all.'

Strictly
QUIZ

If you know your Charleston from your Cha-cha-cha and can conjure up your favourite Strictly Come Dancing moments at the drop of a top hat, our superfan quiz is tailored for you. Keeeeep quizzing …

1. Which two *Strictly* dances are also letters in the NATO phonetic alphabet?

2. Which American girl group did Fleur East pay tribute to in her Blackpool Couple's Choice?

3. Which couple's *Moulin Rouge* Paso Doble landed the first perfect score of series 21?

4. Which celebrity was painted green for a *Wicked*-ly wonderful Tango to 'Defying Gravity' in 2014?

5. Partnered with Oti Mabuse, which *Emmerdale* star lifted the Glitterball trophy in 2018?

6. Which winner dressed up as a *Despicable Me* minion for her energetic Jive?

7. Which series-21 contestant also presented *Come Dancing* in the 1990s?

8. Originating in the nightclubs of America, which Latin dance was popularised in the 1930s when mentioned in a dictionary by bandleader Cab Calloway and became the first *Strictly* dance to score a perfect 40?

9. Which two judges morphed into Morticia and Gomez Addams for the 2022 Halloween special?

10. This year, JB Gill is hoping for a shot at the Glitterball trophy – but which other member of JLS danced on the *Strictly* floor in 2017?

11. In 2013, the show moved into their new studio at Elstree. But where was it filmed before that?

12. Which *Great British Bake Off* star was runner-up in the 2021 Grand Final?

13. Can you name the Scottish comedian who flew down on a dragon for her *Game of Thrones*-themed Foxtrot in series 15?

14. Which Girls Aloud star jumped through a paper hoop after it went up in flames in her series-10 showdance?

15. What anniversary was celebrated with a TV theme tunes special in 2022?

Now in her third series as a *Strictly Come Dancing* professional, Lauren Oakley is looking forward to another exciting year and reckons there are some future dance stars in the new line-up.

'There are some amazing people in the new cast,' she says. 'It's a really good line-up, but more importantly everyone seems happy, keen and ready to work hard. Quite a few are showing some promise. On the day where we first meet them and dance with everybody, there were so many that I thought had loads of potential. They were picking up choreography quickly, which is a great start, because then you can work on the performance and the dancing. I think it's going to be a great series.'

Lauren says the launch show, celebrating the twentieth anniversary, set the tone for another joyous series.

'The launch show was so colourful, so happy, and there were so many throwback songs that everyone recognised,' she says. 'It was just a really good vibe, and the cast seemed super excited. Watching them do the group routine, you are already rooting for them because everyone's so excited to be there.'

Birmingham-born Lauren began dancing at two years old and competing at seven, winning her first world championship at the age of nine. She is two-time winner of the UK Under 21 Latin Championship and has been crowned British Under 21 Latin Champion and British Under 21 Ballroom Champion. After turning professional, she toured the world before joining *Strictly* in 2022. Last year, she partnered newsreader Krishnan Guru-Murthy, making it to week eight.

'Krishnan and I had the best time,' she says. 'Viewers could see his development. He discovered dance and re-discovered a side to himself. It was brilliant to watch him embrace every moment and grow in confidence.'

Krishnan's joy on the dance floor won him an army of fans, and Lauren says she set out to unleash that fun side from the start.

'I loved our Charleston in week three because that was the breakthrough week for him, personally, but my favourite dance with Krishnan was the Quickstep,' she says. 'At the end of the routine the audience were on their feet and I could see the elation in him. It was the most amazing moment and captured everything *Strictly* is about for me.'

Although not partnered with a celebrity this year, Lauren is excited about taking part in the new series and supporting the couples throughout.

'Having been in the competition last year, I'm looking forward to seeing everybody's journey this series, but from the other side,' she says. 'When you're in the competition, you're so focused on what you have to do and on helping your celebrity, so it will be nice to be able to support everybody from outside the competition.'

'I'm also looking forward to the group dances. Movie Week is going to be amazing and, in Blackpool week, I have a special part in the group number, so I'm particularly looking forward to that. I'm excited for what's in store.'

Lauren **Oakley**

Answers

Take 20

1. Kelvin Fletcher **T**
2. Aljaž Škorjanec **G**
3. Ore Aduba **L**
4. Darren Gough **F**
5. Oti Mabuse **E**
6. Natasha Kaplinsky **Q**
7. Matt Dawson **R**
8. Aliona Vilani **M**
9. Louis Smith **C**

10. Katya Jones **J**
11. Denise Lewis **N**
12. Pamela Stephenson **B**
13. Zoe Ball **D**
14. Tom Chambers **S**
15. Harry Judd **O**
16. Gethin Jones **K**
17. Stacey Dooley **P**
18. John Whaite **I**
19. Amy Dowden **A**
20. Bill Bailey **H**

Answers
Word SEARCH

X	L	E	A	D	E	R	B	O	A	R	D	D	S	C
S	A	M	B	A	B	N	M	V	I	C	V	L	A	G
R	D	O	O	M	O	Y	R	O	T	K	C	B	O	L
A	W	Q	U	T	R	P	H	O	I	N	E	G	J	L
W	O	P	L	K	S	C	A	N	L	O	N	U	P	E
D	A	E	F	E	C	I	X	M	P	A	L	L	I	W
N	K	A	R	I	M	K	M	J	T	L	K	Q	Y	S
S	R	M	A	R	Q	U	M	A	N	R	A	R	A	U
O	O	X	R	E	I	Z	A	R	B	Y	B	B	O	B
I	G	W	I	L	F	A	B	R	K	U	G	T	V	E
N	O	C	K	S	T	R	A	U	S	Q	S	B	O	N
C	N	N	O	T	R	A	B	A	M	M	E	E	K	N
P	I	X	V	R	O	G	K	F	U	I	K	D	U	A
T	K	T	F	E	X	J	U	I	C	H	M	U	O	I
R	K	A	R	E	N	H	A	U	E	R	P	Q	P	D
G	B	W	A	O	G	H	B	I	L	D	P	A	I	L

Answers QUIZ

1. Tango and Foxtrot

2. Destiny's Child

3. Layton and Nikita

4. Frankie Bridge

5. Kelvin Fletcher

6. Stacey Dooley

7. Angela Rippon

8. The Jive

9. Craig Revel Horwood
(Morticia) and Shirley
Ballas (Gomez)

10. Aston Merrygold

11. BBC Television Centre,
West London

12. John Whaite

13. Susan Calman

14. Kimberley Walsh

15. The centenary
(100 years) of the BBC

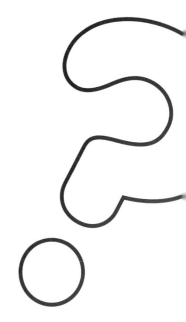